OVER 100 QUICK-FIX, GLUTEN-FREE RECIPES

Melissa Petitto, R.D.

Race Point Publishing
An imprint of Quarto Publishing Group USA Inc.
276 Fifth Avenue, Suite 205
New York, NY 10001

RACE POINT PUBLISHING and the distinctive Race Point Publishing logo are trademarks of the Quarto Publishing Group USA Inc.

ISBN: 978-1-937994-54-9

Library of Congress Cataloging-in-Publication Data is available

Art Direction by Heidi North
Interior Design by Leah Lococo
Food Stylist: Suzanne Lenzer
Assistant Food Stylist: Michaela Hayes
Prop Stylist: Glynis Cotton

Printed in China

1 3 5 7 9 10 8 6 4 2

ACKNOWLEDGMENTS

To Brian, my love and best friend, thank you for tasting and honestly critiquing each and every one of the recipes in this book. It was a hard job and you did it with gusto!

TABLE OF CONTENTS

FOREWORD

I came to find out about the Paleo diet at CrossFit Virtuosity in Brooklyn, New York. It all sounded a little crazy at the time, especially when the trainer, Kurt Tullar, told me, "Milk is great, if you're a baby cow."

Fast-forward three years, and I'm writing the foreword to a Paleo cookbook. And every time I see a glass of milk, I think, "That's great…if you're a baby cow."

I would like to tell you that I've been a paragon of Paleo-ness. That I pre-plan a week's worth of meals every Sunday, eat only free-range meat, and can't remember the last time I ingested wheat. But I would be lying. The truth is, like many of you, I constantly struggle to filter the crap out of my diet. It's not just a struggle with myself, but a battle against the grain of society. No matter how many pseudo-healthy foods creep onto store shelves, the idea that we will each eat more than 3,000 calories of horrifying chemical goo per day is as American as apple pie made with partially hydrogenated soybean oil.

Paleo practitioners are caught between long work days in offices full of sugary junk food, miles-long stretches of restaurants that almost exclusively serve GMO foods, and meals from our grandmothers lovingly made with enough gut-busting sugar and cheese to make us hate ourselves for weeks.

With very little to support us aside from each other, being Paleo requires both discipline and logistical finesse. And that's assuming you've found Paleo foods that you like in the first place; evidently, man cannot subsist on bacon alone (though I refute this). The best place to be Paleo is in your own kitchen, cooking foods from fresh ingredients that have never seen the inside of a commercial food factory.

So I was thrilled to find out that Melissa was working on this 30-minute recipe collection—and helping to improve our Paleo logistical problems. Quality-wise, these recipes are good enough to bamboozle even those with normal diets into enjoying Paleo foods. Melissa, a bona fide dietician and personal chef to the rich and famous, has applied her expertise to our culinary niche—and the results are tasty.

And now, thanks to her, the list of excuses that we Paleo disciples can give for screwing up our diets grows even smaller. So, read on, and enjoy! Stick to your diets, and stay healthy.

—BRYAN HARRIS,
Paleo devotee, published author,
and health writer

INTRODUCTION

As a personal chef, Registered Dietitian, and cookbook author, I thought I had seen every diet and food lifestyle out there…until I was introduced to the Paleo diet through a private client who is an avid devotee. In crafting fresh, Paleo-friendly meals for her, I became familiar not only with the delicious ingredients, but also with the close-knit group of people who love their workouts, love their food, and tie the two together by being mindful and honest about how they nourish themselves.

As an avid lifetime athlete myself—a ballerina until I was seventeen, and now a devoted yogi—I am a firm believer in being thoughtful about how we choose to eat and mindful about what we put into our bodies. When I first started creating recipes for this book, I thought the difficulty would be in the exclusion of ingredients like grains, legumes, dairy, refined salt and sugars, and processed oils. I could not have been more wrong! The Paleo diet, consisting mainly of fish and seafood, grass–fed and pasture-raised meats, eggs, fruits, vegetables, and nuts and seeds is such a rich platform for foodies and Paleo followers alike that I found myself loving each and every one of the recipes I was creating.

The biggest challenge in creating this cookbook ended up coming down to the 30-minute time restriction. When researching the traditional Paleo recipe, I found them to be time-consuming, which to me means that finding time to create those foods to nourish your body on a day-to-day basis is nearly impossible. I truly hope my book helps bridge the gap between loving how you feel and look on the Paleo diet and finding the time to cook this way every day for you and your family.

When shopping for Paleo-friendly ingredients and developing the recipes for this book, the farmers' market was my go-to stop. Not only are you sure to find all the locally sourced meat and seafood your heart desires, but you also get to utilize the abundance of seasonal and organic produce which is optimal for the highest vitamin and nutrient content…not to mention the best taste!

If *30-Minute Paleo Meals* makes it easier to stick to your plan, then I know I've done my job! I hope you're hungry…

—MELISSA PETITTO

KEY INGREDIENTS

If you want to successfully make delicious, 30-minute recipes on the Paleo diet, it's important to keep your shelves stocked with these key ingredients that I use throughout the book:

FATS

Coconut Butter
Coconut Oil
Extra-virgin Olive Oil
Grass-fed Butter
Sesame Oil

VINEGARS AND FLAVORINGS

Balsamic Vinegar
Coconut Aminos
Fish Sauce (a Paleo-friendly brand)
Grade B Maple Syrup
Herbs
Mustard
Raw Honey
Sea Salt
Spices
Unfiltered Apple Cider Vinegar

NUTS AND SEEDS

Almond Butter
Almonds
Cashew Butter
Cashews
Hazelnut Butter
Hazelnuts
Macadamia Nut Butter
Macadamia Nuts
Pecans
Pine Nuts
Pumpkin Seeds
Sunflower Seed Butter
Sunflower Seeds
Walnuts

FLOURS AND BAKING INGREDIENTS

Almond Meal Flour
Almond Milk
Arrowroot Powder
Coconut Flour
Coconut Milk
Unsweetened Flaked Coconut

CHEF'S NOTES

- Unless otherwise stated, eggs are assumed to be large. Also, use the freshest eggs possible.
- Unless otherwise stated, individual vegetables and fruits are assumed to be medium. All citrus fruits should be unwaxed when zest is required.
- All herbs are assumed to be fresh.
- Cooking times are for guidance only, as individual ovens vary. If you are based in the UK and using a fan oven, please follow the manufacturer's instructions concerning oven temperatures.
- Some recipes include raw or very lightly cooked eggs or meat. These should be avoided particularly by the elderly, infants, pregnant women, convalescents, and anyone with an impaired immune system. If you're not sure about using a recipe, please consult with your doctor.
- Both metric and imperial measurements are used in the book. Follow one set of measurements throughout, not a mixture, as they are not interchangeable.
- All spoon measurements are level unless otherwise stated. If you are based in Australia, the Australian standard tablespoons are 20ml. Australian readers are advised to use 3 teaspoons in place of 1 tablespoon when measuring small quantities.
- Some recipes call for baking powder, but baking powder is not Paleo-friendly. As a substitute, combine baking soda and cream of tartar in the following quantities, then add it in where baking powder is called for in the recipe:
  ½ teaspoon baking powder = ⅛ teaspoon baking soda + ¼ teaspoon cream of tartar
  1 teaspoon baking powder = ¼ teaspoon baking soda + ½ teaspoon cream of tartar

OVEN TEMPERATURE CONVERSIONS

°F	°C	Gas Mark
300°F	150°C	2
325°F	160°C	3
350°F	180°C	4
375°F	190°C	5
400°F	200°C	6
425°F	220°C	7
450°F	230°C	8
475°F	240°C	9

CHAPTER 1

BREAK-FAST

BANANA BREAD FRENCH TOAST

This recipe is so incredibly amazing and easy—you can even save time by freezing a few loaves of banana bread and defrosting them as needed. Use your imagination to create different variations, such as banana and bacon French toast. Serve with butter and pure maple syrup or fresh fruit for an awesome breakfast!

▶ Preparation Time: 5 minutes | Cooking Time: 10–16 minutes | Total Time: 15–21 minutes | SERVES 4

1 loaf Banana Bread (page 181), cut into ½" (1.3cm)-thick slices
3 organic free-range eggs
¼ cup (60ml/2fl oz) unsweetened almond or coconut milk
1 teaspoon ground cinnamon
¼ teaspoon sea salt
2 tablespoons coconut oil or bacon grease
butter and maple syrup, to serve

1. Preheat a griddle over medium heat.
2. In a medium bowl, combine the eggs, almond or coconut milk, cinnamon, and salt and mix well.
3. Add the coconut oil or bacon grease to the griddle.
4. Carefully dip the slices of banana bread into the egg mixture, coating both sides, and then place them on the griddle.
5. Cook for 2–4 minutes on first side, then flip and cook for another 3–4 minutes.
6. Remove from the pan to a plate. Serve with butter and maple syrup.

CAL 700 | CAL FROM FAT 450 | TOTAL FAT 31G | SAT FAT 15G | SODIUM 415MG | FIBER 5G | PRO 13G

BLUEBERRY MUFFINS

Seriously so quick and delicious! Whether prepared in advance or in the morning, these amazing muffins taste best straight out of the oven.

▶ Preparation Time: 10 minutes | Cooking Time: 15–20 minutes | Total Time: 25–30 minutes | MAKES 12

1 cup (240g/8½oz) unsalted almond butter
3 organic free-range eggs
½ cup (120ml/6fl oz) raw honey
⅓ cup (75ml/2¾fl oz) coconut oil
1 cup (100g/3½oz) almond meal
⅓ cup (25g/1oz) unsweetened shredded coconut
2 tablespoons ground flax meal
½ teaspoon baking soda
½ teaspoon baking powder (page 9)
¼ teaspoon sea salt
¼ teaspoon ground cinnamon
⅛ teaspoon freshly ground nutmeg
½ cup (70g/2½oz) fresh blueberries or your favorite berries
½ cup (65g/2¼oz) chopped walnuts, toasted (optional)

1. Preheat the oven to 350°F. Line a 12-cup muffin tin with 12 paper muffin liners.
2. In a large bowl, combine the almond butter, eggs, honey, and coconut oil. With a handheld mixer on medium speed, mix for 2–3 minutes, or until well combined. Set aside.
3. In a separate bowl, combine the almond meal, coconut, flax meal, baking soda, baking powder, salt, cinnamon and nutmeg and mix well.
4. Add the dry ingredients into the wet and stir until just combined. Do not overmix the ingredients—the muffins will be tough and won't rise properly.
5. Fold in the blueberries and chopped walnuts, if using.
6. Spoon the batter into each muffin liner, about three-quarters full.
7. Bake in the oven for 15–20 minutes, or until risen and golden.

CAL 320 | CAL FROM FAT 220 | TOTAL FAT 25G | SAT FAT 8G | SODIUM 180MG | FIBER 4G | PRO 8G

GREEN SMOOTHIE

What breakfast could be more complete with protein, vitamin A, vitamin K, calcium, iron, dietary fiber, and omega-3s? Thick, creamy, and filling, this morning pick-me-up is packed with nutrients and tastes utterly divine.

▶ Preparation Time: 5 minutes | Cooking Time: 0 minutes | Total Time: 5 minutes | SERVES 2

¾ cup (175 ml/6fl oz) unsweetened almond milk
½ cup (15g/½ oz) baby spinach, packed
½ cup (30g/1oz) kale, packed
1 avocado, halved, pitted, and flesh scooped out
1 cucumber, halved
1 Fuji apple, cored and quartered
1 tablespoon raw honey
1 teaspoon ground flax

1. Add all the ingredients to a blender and process until smooth.

CAL 280 | CAL FROM FAT 150 | TOTAL FAT 16G | SAT FAT 2G | SODIUM 95MG | FIBER 11G | PRO 5G

BAKED EGGS WITH PORTOBELLO MUSHROOM, PANCETTA & KALE

Start off the day with a delicious and nutritious breakfast that's super easy and beautiful! Go easy on the seasoning of your eggs because of the sodium content in the pancetta.

▶ Preparation Time: 8 minutes | Cooking Time: 18–22 minutes | Total Time: 26–30 minutes | SERVES 4

1 teaspoon olive oil
4 large portobello mushrooms, cleaned, stemmed, and gills scraped out
4 thin slices pancetta
1 cup (65g/2oz) baby kale
4 organic free-range eggs
¼ teaspoon sea salt
1 teaspoon freshly ground black pepper
1 tablespoon chopped parsley

1. Preheat the oven to 400°F. Line a baking sheet with parchment paper.
2. Rub olive oil on the outside of the prepared mushroom caps and place them flat on the baking sheet.
3. Place a slice of pancetta and ¼ cup (16g) of baby kale inside each mushroom cap.
4. Crack an egg into a small bowl and then carefully slide it into a pancetta-and-kale-filled mushroom cap. Repeat with the remaining eggs.
5. Season with salt and pepper. Sprinkle the parsley on top.
6. Bake in the oven for 18–22 minutes, depending on how you like your eggs cooked.

CAL 170 | CAL FROM FAT 80 | TOTAL FAT 9G | SAT FAT 3G | SODIUM 970 MG | FIBER 1G | PRO 17G

MINI PROSCIUTTO-WRAPPED SPINACH FRITTATAS

Advanced preparations do wonders for a busy schedule. This is an easy and divine dish to prepare the night before, reheat in the morning, and take to go! It's perfectly packed with everything you need to start the day off right. The prosciutto has a high salt content, so use the sea salt sparingly when you season.

▶ Preparation Time: 5 minutes | Cooking Time: 22–25 minutes | Total Time: 27–30 minutes | SERVES 6

1 tablespoon coconut oil, olive oil, or bacon fat
12 thin slices prosciutto
1 x 10oz (284g) package frozen chopped spinach, thawed and squeezed dry
8 organic free-range eggs
2 garlic cloves, minced
¼ cup (60ml/2fl oz) unsweetened coconut or almond milk
2 tablespoons coconut flour
¼ teaspoon sea salt
1 teaspoon freshly ground black pepper

1. Preheat the oven to 400°F. Grease a 12-cup muffin tin with the oil or bacon fat.
2. Line each muffin cup with a slice of prosciutto, making sure to cover the bottom and sides completely. Set aside.
3. In a large bowl, combine the spinach, eggs, garlic, coconut or almond milk, and coconut flour and whisk until combined and fluffy. Season with salt and pepper.
4. Spoon the frittata batter into each prosciutto-filled muffin cup. Bake in the oven for 22–25 minutes, or until puffed and the eggs are cooked through.

CAL 230 | CAL FROM FAT 110 | TOTAL FAT 13G | SAT FAT 5G | SODIUM 750MG | FIBER 4G | PRO 17G

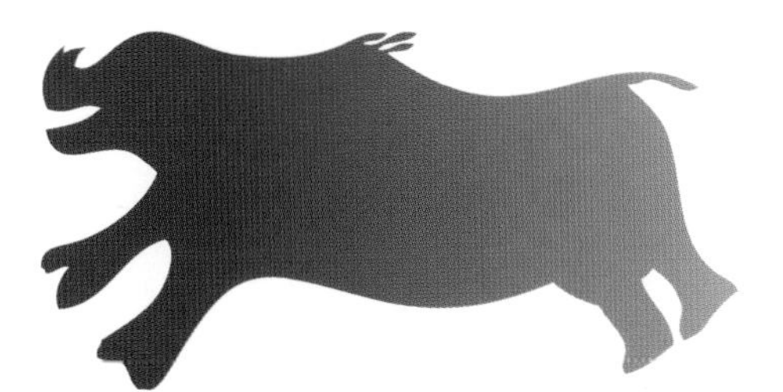

SMOKED SALMON & ASPARAGUS FRITTATA

I love frittatas, and the salmon paired with the asparagus makes a wonderful combination in this dish. If you're looking to add something fresh, simply top off the frittata with avocado or chopped tomatoes.

▶ Preparation Time: 10 minutes | Cooking Time: 9–13 minutes | Total Time: 19–23 minutes | SERVES 6

1 tablespoon olive oil
1 large sweet onion, diced
1lb (450g/16oz) asparagus, trimmed and cut into 1" (2.5cm) pieces
12 organic free-range eggs
¼ cup (60ml/2fl oz) filtered water
1 teaspoon grated lemon zest
2 tablespoons dill, chopped
½ teaspoon sea salt
1 teaspoon freshly ground black pepper
8oz (230g) smoked salmon, roughly chopped

1. Preheat the oven to broil.
2. Heat the oil in a large nonstick, ovenproof pan over medium-high heat. Add the onion and sauté for 3–5 minutes, stirring occasionally.
3. Add the asparagus and sauté for an additional 2–3 minutes, or until bright green and crisp-tender.
4. In a large bowl, combine the eggs, water, lemon zest, dill, salt, and pepper and whisk until lightly frothy.
5. Stir in the smoked salmon.
6. Once the asparagus is cooked, pour the egg mixture into the pan and reduce the heat to medium.
7. Using a rubber spatula, pull the egg from the sides of the pan into the center, helping the egg mixture to cook evenly. Cook over medium heat for 3 minutes longer, or until beginning to set.
8. Transfer the pan to the broiler and broil for 1–2 minutes until set and lightly browned on top.
9. Carefully flip the frittata onto a large plate and cut into 12 pieces. Serve hot or at room temperature.

CAL 220 | CAL FROM FAT 120 | TOTAL FAT 14G | SAT FAT 4G | SODIUM 600MG | FIBER 0G | PRO 20G

TOMATO & BASIL BAKED EGGS

Make this elegant and super-simple dish during the summer when tomatoes are at their best. You can always add extra greens such as spinach, kale, or baby mustard greens to boost the nutritional content.

▶ Preparation Time: 5 minutes | Cooking Time: 20–25 minutes | Total Time: 25–30 minutes | SERVES 4

4 large globe tomatoes
1 teaspoon sea salt, divided
1 teaspoon freshly ground black pepper, divided
4 large basil leaves
4 organic free-range eggs

1. Preheat the oven to 450°F. Line an 8" (20cm)-square baking pan with parchment paper or aluminum foil.
2. Cut about ¼" (6mm) off the top of each tomato. Using a melon baller, spoon, or ice-cream scoop, remove the seeds and flesh from inside the tomato, making sure not to cut into the sides. If your tomato does not sit flat on its own, slice a very small piece off the bottom so that it does. Repeat with remaining tomatoes.
3. Season the inside of each tomato with half of the salt and pepper. Add a basil leaf inside each tomato, then place into the prepared baking pan.
4. Crack an egg into each tomato cavity and season with the remaining salt and pepper.
5. Bake in the oven for 20–25 minutes, depending on how you like your eggs cooked.

CAL 110 | CAL FROM FAT 45 | TOTAL FAT 5G | SAT FAT 1.5G | SODIUM 560MG | FIBER 1G | PRO 7G

CARROT & ALMOND BUTTER MUFFINS

These filling muffins make a yummy on-the-go breakfast. Packed with fresh vegetables, fruit, and almond butter, one muffin is sure to keep you full for whatever your morning entails.

▶ Preparation Time: 5 minutes | Cooking Time: 23–25 minutes | Total Time: 28–30 minutes | MAKES 12

6 carrots, finely shredded
⅔ cup (165g/6oz) unsalted almond butter
1 organic free-range egg
¼ cup (60ml/2fl oz) applesauce
3 tablespoons raw honey
1 tablespoon ground cinnamon
½ teaspoon baking powder (page 9)
¼ teaspoon sea salt
½ cup (80g/3oz) golden raisins

1. Preheat the oven to 375°F. Line a 12-cup muffin tin with 12 paper muffin liners.
2. In a large bowl, combine the carrots, almond butter, egg, applesauce, and honey and mix well.
3. Stir in the cinnamon, baking powder, and salt and mix until just combined.
4. Fold in the raisins.
5. Spoon the batter into the prepared muffin tin, filling each cup halfway. Bake for 23–25 minutes, or until a toothpick inserted into the center of a muffin comes out clean.

CAL 140 | CAL FROM FAT 80 | TOTAL FAT 8G | SAT FAT 0.5G | SODIUM 115MG | FIBER 3G | PRO 4G

WAFFLES WITH WILD BOAR SAUSAGE, SWEET POTATO, BABY KALE RAGOUT & MAPLE SYRUP

If you love breakfast for dinner, this is your recipe! If you can't find wild boar sausage, you can easily swap for pork sausage.

▶ Preparation Time: 8 minutes | Cooking Time: 22 minutes | Total Time: 30 minutes | SERVES 8

olive oil or coconut oil spray
1 Honeycrisp or Gala apple, cored and quartered
1 banana, roughly chopped
1 cup (250g/9oz) unsalted almond butter
2 organic free-range eggs
1 tablespoon arrowroot
½ teaspoon baking soda
½ teaspoon sea salt

FOR THE RAGOUT
1 tablespoon olive oil or duck fat
2 large sweet onions, diced
1 Granny Smith apple, cored and diced
1lb (450g/16oz) wild boar sausage meat
1 teaspoon crushed red pepper flakes
1 teaspoon ground cinnamon
½ teaspoon sea salt
3 cups (200g/7oz) baby kale, washed and dried
grade B maple syrup, to serve

1. Spray the waffle iron with olive or coconut oil and preheat.
2. In a blender or food processor, combine the apple, banana, almond butter, eggs, arrowroot, baking soda, and salt and puree until smooth and creamy. Set aside.
3. In the meantime, make the ragout. Heat the olive oil or duck fat in a large sauté pan over medium-high heat. Add the onions and apple and sauté for 3 minutes, or until softened.
4. Pour ¼ cup (60ml) of the waffle batter into each side of the waffle maker, making sure not to add too much so that it overflows. Cook until golden, about 2–3 minutes per batch. Keep the cooked waffles warm while you repeat with the remaining batter.
5. To the ragout in the pan, add the sausage meat, crushed red pepper flakes, cinnamon, and salt and sauté for another 3–5 minutes, or until the sausage meat is cooked through, stirring and breaking up the sausage meat occasionally. Add the baby kale and stir until just wilted.
6. To serve, top the warm waffles with the ragout and accompany with maple syrup. Delicious!

CAL 510 | CAL FROM FAT 330 | TOTAL FAT 37G | SAT FAT 8G | SODIUM 790MG | FIBER 6G | PRO 20G

BLUEBERRY ALMOND PANCAKES

This is the ultimate comfort breakfast for the Paleo lifestyle. Mix it up by adding your own favorite toppings.

▶ Preparation Time: 2 minutes | Cooking Time: 6–12 minutes | Total Time: 8–14 minutes
MAKES 12 SMALL PANCAKES

coconut oil spray
1½ cups (150g/5¼oz) almond meal
4 organic free-range eggs
¼ cup (60ml/2fl oz) unsweetened almond or coconut milk
¼ cup (60ml/2fl oz) coconut oil
1 tablespoon raw honey
½ teaspoon sea salt
½ teaspoon gluten-free baking powder (page 9)
1 cup (140g/5oz) blueberries
butter, to serve
grade B maple syrup, to serve

1. Heat a griddle pan over medium heat and spray with coconut oil.
2. Add all the ingredients except berries to a blender or food processor and process until smooth.
   Fold in the fresh blueberries.
3. Once the griddle is heated, ladle a scant ¼ cup (60ml) of batter and cook for 1–2 minutes, or until the top begins to bubble. Flip the pancake and cook for another 1–2 minutes, or until golden. Repeat with the rest of the batter.
4. Serve immediately with butter and maple syrup.

CAL 540 | CAL FROM FAT 440 | TOTAL FAT 49G | SAT FAT 12G | SODIUM 400MG | FIBER 7G | PRO 18G

CHAPTER 2

SWEET POTATO, EGG & BACON SALAD

Salads are summer barbecue essentials, and this side dish is perfect for groups. The combination of potato, egg, and bacon is a natural one, but the twist of sweet potato instead of white potato makes this salad a Paleo no-brainer!

▶ Preparation Time: 5 minutes | Cooking Time: 19–23 minutes | Total Time: 24–28 minutes | SERVES 6

4 organic free-range eggs
2 sweet potatoes, peeled and diced into ½" (1.3cm) pieces
5 slices bacon, cooked and crumbled, plus 1 tablespoon fat reserved
½ teaspoon sea salt

FOR THE SAUCE

½ sweet onion, diced
1 scallion, chopped
¼ cup (60ml/2fl oz) Homemade Mayonnaise (page 187)
2 tablespoons Whole-Grain Mustard (page 191)
2 tablespoons unfiltered apple cider vinegar

1. Preheat the oven to 425°F. Line a baking sheet with aluminum foil.
2. Place eggs in a medium saucepan and cover with cold water. Bring to a boil over high heat, then reduce heat to medium-high and boil for 7 minutes.
3. In a medium bowl, combine the sweet potato, reserved bacon fat, and salt. Stir to coat, then transfer to the prepared baking sheet.
4. Bake in the oven for 15–17 minutes, or until tender and slightly browned. Once cooked, allow to cool for 2–3 minutes.
5. To make the sauce, combine the onion, scallion, mayonnaise, mustard, and apple cider vinegar in a large bowl. Mix well and set aside.
6. Drain the eggs and cover with cold water and ice. Allow to cool for 2–3 minutes, or until cool enough to handle. Peel, chop, and then add to the mayonnaise sauce.
7. Add the potatoes to the mixture and toss just to combine. Top with crumbled bacon and serve.

CAL 230 | CAL FROM FAT 130 | TOTAL FAT 14G | SAT FAT 3.5G | SODIUM 360MG | FIBER 3G | PROTEIN 7G

GRILLED CHICKEN, WILD ARUGULA, ASIAN PEAR & WALNUT SALAD WITH WALNUT VINAIGRETTE

This quick, delicious, and hearty salad is a great way to use up extra grilled chicken! Peppery fresh arugula, crispy and lightly sweet Asian pear, earthy and creamy walnuts—you can't beat this tasty, substantial main-dish salad.

▶ Preparation Time: 15 minutes | Cooking Time: 15 minutes | Total Time: 30 minutes | SERVES 4

- 4 x 5oz (150g) boneless, skinless free-range chicken breasts
- 1 tablespoon olive oil
- ½ teaspoon sea salt
- 1 teaspoon freshly ground black pepper
- 4 cups (80g/30oz) wild baby arugula
- 1 Asian pear, julienned and kept in lemon water
- ¼ cup (25g/1oz) walnuts, toasted and chopped
- ½ pomegranate, seeds only

FOR THE DRESSING

- ¼ cup (60ml/2fl oz) unfiltered apple cider vinegar
- 1 tablespoon Whole-Grain Mustard (page 191)
- 1 teaspoon raw honey
- ¼ teaspoon sea salt
- ¼ teaspoon freshly ground black pepper
- ¼ cup (60ml/2fl oz) walnut oil

1. Preheat a grill or indoor grill pan over high heat.
2. In a medium bowl, combine the chicken breasts, olive oil, salt, and pepper and toss to coat. Grill for 4–5 minutes on each side, or until completely cooked through. Transfer to a cutting board and allow to cool for 1–2 minutes. Slice on the bias, then set aside.
3. To make the dressing, in a small bowl, combine the apple cider vinegar, mustard, honey, salt, and pepper and mix well. Slowly drizzle in the walnut oil, whisking continuously to thoroughly combine. Set aside.
4. To assemble the salad, arrange 1 cup (20g) arugula on a plate. Drain the Asian pear and place one-quarter of slices over the arugula. Sprinkle on 1 tablespoon walnuts, 1 tablespoon pomegranate seeds, and top with 1 sliced chicken breast. Repeat with the other three plates. Drizzle with the dressing and serve.

CAL 380 | CAL FROM FAT 230 | TOTAL FAT 25G | SAT FAT 3G | SODIUM 500MG | FIBER 4G | PRO 26G

WATERMELON & TOMATO GAZPACHO WITH PICKLED RED ONIONS & JALAPEÑOS

Gazpacho makes use of all the seasonable vegetables in summer, and this amazing recipe is no exception. Fresh, slightly acidic, spicy, and abounding with flavor, it's truly summer in a bowl.

▶ Preparation Time: 20 minutes | Cooking Time: 0 minutes | Total Time: 20 minutes | SERVES 8

5 cups seedless watermelon, chopped
5 beefsteak tomatoes, cored and chopped
1 English cucumber, roughly chopped
½ cup (20g/¾oz) basil leaves
½ cup (30g/1oz) cilantro leaves
½ cup (20g/¾oz) mint leaves
1 teaspoon sea salt
2 tablespoons sherry vinegar
1 tablespoon olive oil

FOR THE PICKLES

1 jalapeño, thinly sliced
½ red onion, thinly sliced
1 tablespoon coconut crystals
¼ cup (60ml/2fl oz) sherry vinegar
¼ cup (60ml/2fl oz) filtered water

1. To make the pickles, combine the jalapeño, onion, coconut crystals, sherry vinegar, and water in a medium bowl and mix well. Set aside.
2. In a food processor or blender, working in batches, puree the watermelon and tomatoes, until smooth. Repeat until all the watermelon and tomatoes have been pureed. Transfer to a large bowl.
3. In the same food processor or blender, puree the cucumber, basil, cilantro, mint, salt, and vinegar until smooth. With the motor still running, slowly add in the olive oil and continue to process until smooth. Pour this into the watermelon mixture and combine.
4. To serve, ladle the gazpacho into bowls and serve with the pickles.

CAL 70 | CAL FROM FAT 20 | TOTAL FAT 2G | SAT FAT 0G | SODIUM 260MG | FIBER 1G | PRO 2G

CURRIED SQUASH SOUP WITH CRAB

This healthy and delicious soup is packed with flavor, from the sweet and warming squash and the earthy spices to the delicate zest of the crabmeat topping; you will be making this one all the time.

▶ Preparation Time: 3–4 minutes | Cooking Time: 20 minutes | Total Time: 23–24 minutes | SERVES 4

1 butternut squash, peeled and roughly chopped
2 small carrots, roughly chopped
2 garlic cloves, smashed
1" (2.5cm) piece fresh ginger root, peeled and roughly chopped
1 tablespoon curry powder
1 teaspoon turmeric
1 teaspoon ground cumin
1 teaspoon sea salt
2 cups (475ml/16fl oz) chicken broth
1 x 14oz (400ml) can coconut milk
¼ cup (30g/1oz) pistachios, shelled
¼ cup (15g/½oz) cilantro leaves
1 teaspoon orange zest
½ teaspoon freshly ground black pepper
1 cup (225g/8oz) jumbo lump crabmeat, picked over for shells

1. In a large soup pot over medium-high heat, add the butternut squash, carrots, garlic, ginger, curry powder, turmeric, cumin, salt, chicken broth, and coconut milk. Bring to a boil, then reduce heat and simmer for 20 minutes, or until the squash and carrots are tender.
2. While the soup is cooking, place the pistachios, cilantro, orange zest, and pepper in a food processor. Pulse 15–20 times, or until the mixture is finely chopped. Transfer the mixture to a medium bowl and gently fold in the lump crabmeat. Set aside.
3. Transfer the soup to the food processor and puree until smooth.
4. To serve, ladle soup into bowls and top with the crabmeat mixture.

CAL 370 | CAL FROM FAT 230 | TOTAL FAT 26G | SAT FAT 19G | SODIUM 1000MG | FIBER 6G | PRO 20G

WILD ARUGULA SALAD WITH CRISPY DUCK CONFIT, BUTTERNUT SQUASH CROUTONS & AVOCADO DRESSING

This salad also works as a wonderful main dish. Duck confit is a salt-cured duck leg that is slow-braised in its own fat—it makes a luxurious addition to a simple salad and can be purchased from your local butcher. Look for a trusted duck purveyor in your area, and you will thoroughly enjoy this salad.

▶ Preparation Time: 5 minutes | Cooking Time: 15–20 minutes | Total Time: 20–25 minutes | SERVES 4

½ butternut squash, peeled and diced into ½" (1.3cm) pieces
1 teaspoon olive oil
¼ teaspoon sea salt
¼ teaspooon freshly ground pepper
2 duck confit legs
4 cups (80g/3oz) wild arrugula, cleaned and dried

FOR THE DRESSING

1 avocado, halved, pitted, and flesh scooped out
1 jalapeño, stem and seeds removed, roughly chopped
1 garlic clove
juice of 2 limes
¼ cup (60ml/2fl oz) filtered water
2 tablespoons unfiltered apple cider vinegar
¼ cup (10g/⅓oz) basil leaves
1 tablespoon raw honey
¼ teaspoon sea salt
¼ cup (60ml/2fl oz) olive oil

1. Preheat the oven to 425°F. Line two baking sheets with aluminum foil.
2. In a large bowl, combine the butternut squash, olive oil, salt, and pepper and toss well. Arrange the squash in a single layer on a prepared baking sheet. Roast in the oven for 15–20 minutes, or until crispy and tender.
3. Place the duck legs, skin side up, on the other baking sheet. Roast in the oven for 10 minutes, or until the skin is crispy. Allow to cool for 3 minutes, then shred the duck into bite-size pieces. Set aside.
4. To prepare the dressing, combine the avocado, jalapeño, garlic, lime juice, water, apple cider vinegar, basil, honey, and salt in a blender and puree until smooth. Slowly add in the olive oil and puree until well mixed. Set aside.
5. To serve the salad, arrange the butternut squash on a platter, then top with the wild arugula, and shredded duck meat. Spoon the dressing over the top and serve immediately.

CAL 310 | CAL FROM FAT 250 | TOTAL FAT 28G | SAT FAT 5G | SODIUM 280MG | FIBER 6G | PRO 12G

BABY SPINACH SALAD WITH ROASTED TOMATOES, ASPARAGUS & PROSCIUTTO

This simple salad is a colorful and versatile choice for a casual dinner at home or an elegant party.

▶ Preparation Time: 5 minutes | Cooking Time: 25 minutes | Total Time: 30 minutes | SERVES 4

5 Roma tomatoes, tops removed and quartered
1lb (450g/16oz) asparagus, trimmed
4oz (120g) prosciutto, thinly sliced
1 tablespoon olive oil
1 teaspoon sea salt
1 teaspoon freshly ground black pepper
7 cups (210g/8oz) baby spinach

FOR THE DRESSING

3 tablespoons balsamic vinegar
1 tablespoon raw honey
¼ cup (10g/¼oz) basil leaves, thinly sliced
¼ teaspoon sea salt
½ teaspoon freshly ground black pepper
¼ cup (60m/2fl oz) olive oil

1. Preheat the oven to 400°F. Line three baking sheets with aluminum foil.
2. On one baking sheet, arrange the tomatoes cut side up. On another baking sheet, arrange the asparagus in a single layer. On the last baking sheet, arrange the prosciutto in a single layer. Drizzle the tomatoes and asparagus with olive oil and season with salt and pepper.
3. Place the baking sheets in the oven. Bake the prosciutto for 10 minutes, or until crispy; the asparagus for 12–15 minutes, or until just tender; and the tomatoes for 20 minutes.
4. In the meantime, make the dressing. In a small bowl, combine the balsamic vinegar, honey, basil, salt, and pepper and whisk to combine. Slowly drizzle in the olive oil and whisk continuously until thoroughly combined. Set aside.
5. To serve, arrange the spinach on a platter and top with the roasted tomatoes and asparagus. Crumble the prosciutto over each salad and drizzle the basil dressing over the top.

CAL 310 | CAL FROM FAT 200 | TOTAL FAT 22G | SAT FAT 3.5G | SODIUM 1200MG | FIBER 6G | PRO 13G

ROASTED BROCCOLI WITH PINE NUT–PARSLEY PESTO

I love roasted vegetables: The caramelization of sugars creates heightened and complex flavors. This pesto works with asparagus, Brussels sprouts, and most other vegetables, so use it any way you like. If you'd like to prepare some ahead of time, keep it in a sterilized jar in the refrigerator for up to one week.

▶ Preparation Time: 5 minutes | Cooking Time: 15–20 minutes | Total Time: 20–25 minutes | SERVES 6

1 broccoli head, florets only
1 tablespoon olive oil
½ teaspoon sea salt
½ teaspoon freshly ground black pepper

FOR THE PESTO
¼ cup (35g/1oz) pine nuts, toasted
1 cup (60g/2oz) parsley leaves
1 garlic clove
½ teaspoon sea salt
½ teaspoon freshly ground black pepper
¼cup (60ml/2fl oz) olive oil

1. Preheat the oven to 450°F. Line a baking sheet with parchment paper or aluminum foil.
2. In a large bowl, combine the broccoli florets, olive oil, salt, and pepper and toss to coat. Arrange the broccoli on the prepared baking sheet and roast in the oven for 15–20 minutes, or until browned and tender.
3. In the meantime, make the pesto. In a food processor, combine the parsley, pine nuts, garlic, salt, and pepper. Pulse until finely chopped, about 10–15 times. Slowly drizzle in the olive oil and process until incorporated.
4. To serve, drizzle pesto over roasted broccoli and enjoy!

CAL 200 | CAL FROM FAT 160 | TOTAL FAT 18G | SAT FAT 2.5G | SODIUM 370MG | FIBER 4G | PRO 4G

ASIAN CHICKEN SALAD

I tested this recipe with four different people—including men who don't normally like salads—and they adored it! It's not only refreshing and delicious, but it's filling too. Loaded with fresh herbs and vegetables and topped with the bright and creamy Asian Almond Butter Dressing (page 193), it's the perfect treat for lunch or dinner.

▶ Preparation Time: 15 minutes | Cooking Time: 4 minutes | Total Time: 19 minutes
SERVES 4 as a main dish

1 cup (100g/3½oz) French beans
4 cups (80g/3oz) mixed baby greens
1lb (450g/16oz) grilled chicken breast, shredded
3 scallions, thinly sliced
2 red, yellow, or orange bell peppers, thinly sliced
1½ carrots, shredded
½ cucumber, sliced
1 cup (150g/5oz) red grapes, halved
1 cup (120g/4oz) jicama, diced
½ cup (30g/1oz) cilantro leaves
½ cup (20g/¾oz) basil leaves
¼ cup (30g/1¼oz) almonds, toasted
Asian Almond Butter Dressing (page193), to taste

1. Bring a pot of water with a steamer insert to a boil. Once boiling, add the French beans to the steamer, cover, and steam until the beans turn bright green, about 4 minutes.
2. While the beans are steaming, prepare a bowl of ice water. Once the beans are done, transfer them to the ice water bath to stop the cooking. Drain the beans and set aside.
3. On individual plates or one large platter, arrange the greens, then top with shredded chicken and all remaining ingredients.
4. Drizzle with the dressing and serve.

CAL 400 | CAL FROM FAT 150 | TOTAL FAT 16G | SAT FAT 3G | SODIUM 1200MG | FIBER 7G | PRO 36G

ZUCCHINI & LEEK SOUP WITH PROSCIUTTO

So it's the end of summer and there is way too much zucchini left in your CSA...what should you do? Make a huge batch of this amazing soup and freeze it for future enjoyment! This zucchini soup is delicious served hot *or* cold.

▶ Preparation Time: 10 minutes | Cooking Time: 15–17 minutes | Total Time: 25–27 minutes | SERVES 4

4 thin slices prosciutto
1 tablespoon olive oil or bacon fat
2 large leeks, sliced
4 zucchini, roughly chopped
3 garlic cloves, minced
1 teaspoon dried thyme
1 quart, or 4 cups, (950ml/32fl oz) chicken broth
½ teaspoon sea salt
1 teaspoon freshly ground black pepper

1. Preheat the oven to 425°F. Line a baking sheet with aluminum foil.
1. Arrange the prosciutto in a single layer on the prepared baking sheet. Bake for 12–15 minutes, or until browned and crispy. Set aside.
2. Heat the olive oil or bacon fat in a large stockpot over medium-high heat.
3. Add the leeks and sauté 3 minutes, stirring frequently.
4. Add the zucchini, garlic, and thyme and sauté another 2 minutes, stirring occasionally.
5. Add the chicken broth, salt, and pepper and bring to a boil. Reduce the heat to medium low and simmer for 10–12 minutes, or until the zucchini is tender. Remove from heat.
6. Using an immersion blender, puree the soup to your desired consistency.
7. To serve, ladle into bowls and top with crumbled prosciutto.

CAL 110 | CAL FROM FAT 50 | TOTAL FAT 6G | SAT FAT 1G | SODIUM 800MG | FIBER 1G | PRO 6G

TOM YUM SOUP WITH SHRIMP

I love tom yum soup for its spiciness, complexity of flavors, and overall healthiness, and this recipe does not disappoint. The kick of spice is invigorating and creates the perfect balance with the sweet-and-sour flavor.

▶ Preparation Time: 5 minutes | Cooking Time: 10 minutes | Total Time: 15 minutes | SERVES 4

2 cups (475ml/16fl oz) chicken broth
1 cup (240ml/8oz) coconut milk
2 tablespoons chili paste
1 cup (70g/2½oz) button mushrooms, sliced
1 cup (150g/5oz) cherry tomatoes, quartered
3 scallions, thinly sliced
½lb (225g/8oz) medium shrimp, peeled and deveined
¼ cup (60ml/2fl oz) Paleo-friendly fish sauce
grated zest of 2 limes
juice of 1 lime
½ cup (30g/1oz) cilantro leaves, for garnish

1. In a large saucepan, combine the chicken broth, coconut milk, chili paste, mushrooms, tomatoes, and scallions. Bring to a boil, reduce the heat to medium low, and simmer for 7 minutes.
2. Add in the shrimp and cook for another minute.
3. Remove from heat, then stir in the fish sauce, lime zest, and lime juice.
4. To serve, ladle into bowls and garnish with cilantro leaves.

CAL 190 | CAL FROM FAT 120 | TOTAL FAT 13G | SAT FAT 11G | SODIUM 800MG | FIBER 1G | PRO 12G

GRILLED SHRIMP, AVOCADO & TOMATO SALAD

Fresh flavor, great textures, and an element of surprise make this salad unique and fun to prepare. Bacon adds hints of smokiness and saltiness that do wonders for this dish, but it's perfectly delicious without it as well.

▶ Preparation Time: 25 minutes | Cooking Time: 4–6 minutes | Total Time: 29–31 minutes | SERVES 4

juice of 1 small orange
juice of 2 limes
juice of 2 lemons
2 garlic cloves, minced
1 tablespoon Dijon mustard
1 tablespoon raw honey
1 teaspoon sea salt
1 teaspoon freshly ground black pepper
⅓ cup (80ml/2½fl oz) olive oil
1lb (450g/16oz) large shrimp, peeled and deveined
1lb (450g/16oz) baby kale
1 ripe avocado
2 cups (300g/10oz) cherry tomatoes, halved
¼ cup (55g/2oz) pumpkin seeds, roasted
¼ cup (10g/⅓oz) basil leaves
4 x 8" (20cm) wooden skewers, soaked in water for 10 minutes
bacon, cooked and crumbled (optional)

1. In a medium bowl, whisk together the juices, garlic, Dijon, honey, salt, and pepper. While whisking, gradually pour in the olive oil. Transfer half of the vinaigrette to a small bowl and set aside.
2. Add the shrimp to the medium bowl with the remaining vinaigrette and marinate for 15 minutes.
3. Preheat the grill or grill pan to medium heat.
4. While the shrimp is marinating, prepare the salad. Peel, pit, and slice the avocado, then drizzle with a little vinaigrette to prevent browning. On four large plates, arrange the kale, avocado, tomatoes, pumpkin seeds, and basil leaves.
5. Skewer the shrimp and grill for 2–3 minutes per side, or until shrimp are golden brown and cooked through.
6. To serve, top each salad with the grilled shrimp and drizzle with the remaining vinaigrette. If you like, sprinkle crumbled bacon over each salad.

CAL 300 | CAL FROM FAT 90 | TOTAL FAT 9G | SAT FAT 1.5G | SODIUM 1200MG | FIBER 8G | PRO 23G

FRESH TUNA NIÇOISE SALAD

Though traditional Niçoise salad uses canned tuna, I prefer mine with fresh seared tuna, which tastes better and adds elegance to the presentation. The preparation and cook time for this recipe will overlap, but don't worry. . .this phenomenal salad will still be ready in under 30 minutes!

▶ Preparation Time: 15 minutes | Cooking Time: 11–13 minutes | Total Time: 26–28 minutes | SERVES 4

2 cups (225g/80oz) French beans, trimmed
2 organic free-range eggs
1lb (450g/16oz) sushi-grade tuna steak
1 teaspoon sea salt, divided
1 teaspoon freshly ground black pepper, divided
1 tablespoon olive oil
1½ cups (225g/8oz) grape tomatoes, halved
1 red onion, thinly sliced
¼ cup (50g/2oz) Niçoise (or any black olives)
2 tablespoons capers, drained and rinsed
1lb (450g/16oz) mixed baby greens

FOR THE DRESSING
juice of 3 lemons
2 tablespoons Dijon mustard
¼ teaspoon sea salt
¼ teaspoon freshly ground black pepper
¼ cup (60ml/2fl oz) olive oil

1. Bring a pot of water with a steamer insert to a boil. Once the water is boiling, add the beans to the steamer, cover, and steam until the beans turn bright green, about 4 minutes.
2. While the beans are steaming, prepare a bowl of ice water. Once the beans are done transfer them to the ice water bath to stop the cooking. Drain the beans and set aside.
3. In a small saucepan, place the eggs in the bottom, cover with cold water, and bring to a boil. Boil for 7 minutes. Drain and cover with ice water for 2 minutes. Drain again, peel, slice thinly, and season with a little salt and pepper. Set aside.
4. To cook the tuna, season both sides with ½ teaspoon each salt pepper.
5. Heat the oil in a sauté pan over high heat. Add the seasoned tuna and sear for 2–3 minutes per side, or until cooked to your desired doneness. Transfer to a cutting board and let sit for 2 minutes before slicing. Slice the tuna thinly against the grain.
6. To make the dressing, whisk together the lemon juice, Dijon, salt, and pepper. Slowly drizzle in the olive oil and whisk until well combined.
7. To prepare the salads, divide the lettuce among four plates, then continue with the French beans, tomatoes, onion, olives, and capers. Top with the sliced egg, and sliced tuna and drizzle with vinaigrette.

CAL 450 | CAL FROM FAT 260 | TOTAL FAT 29G | SAT FAT 5G | SODIUM 1000MG | FIBER 3G | PRO 32G

CRAB, GREEN MANGO, CUCUMBER & COCONUT SALAD WITH CHILI LIME DRESSING

Thai Cuisine combines sweet, sour, salty, and spicy flavors so well! This salad creates such a beautiful balance with the sweet crab, tart green mango, sour lime, and spicy chili; plus it's super healthy and beautiful!

▶ Preparation Time: 20 minutes | Cooking Time: 0 minutes | Total Time: 20 minutes | SERVES 4

1lb (450g/16oz) jumbo lump crabmeat, picked over for shells
2 large green mangoes, finely julienned
2 large cucumbers, seeded and finely julienned
6 cups (200g/7oz) watercress
½ cup (20g/¾oz) basil leaves, thinly sliced
½ cup (20g/¾oz) mint leaves, thinly sliced
½ cup (30g/1oz) cilantro leaves
3 to 4 scallions, thinly sliced
¼ cup (15g/½oz) unsweetened flaked coconut, toasted

FOR THE DRESSING
1 shallot, minced
1 to 2 tablespoons chili paste
1 tablespoon raw honey
2 tablespoons Paleo-friendly fish sauce
juice of 4 limes
¼ cup (60ml/2fl oz) sesame oil

1. For the dressing, whisk together the shallot, chili paste, honey, fish sauce, and lime juice in a large bowl. Slowly drizzle in the sesame oil and whisk to combine.
2. Add in the crab, mango, and cucumbers and gently toss to coat and avoid breaking up the crabmeat too much.
3. On a large platter, arrange the watercress. Top with the dressed crab mixture, basil, mint, cilantro, scallions, and coconut. Serve immediately.

CAL 420 | CAL FROM FAT 150 | TOTAL FAT 18G | SAT FAT 3.5G | SODIUM 1000MG | FIBER 5G | PRO 30G

THAI BEEF SALAD

You'll need to work efficiently to speed up the preparation process here: Prepare the salad while the steak marinates, grills, and rests. But trust me, it's worth it!

▶ Preparation Time: 10 minutes | Cooking Time: 10 minutes | Total Time: 20 minutes | SERVES 4

1lb (450g/16oz) organic grass-fed flank steak
3 tablespoons lime juice
3 tablespoons coconut aminos
2 tablespoons raw honey
2 tablespoons chili paste
2 garlic cloves, minced
1 teaspoon fresh ginger root, minced
1 head butter lettuce, chopped
1 avocado, peeled, pitted, and sliced
1 English cucumber, thinly sliced
1 small red onion, thinly sliced
4 scallions, sliced
½ cup (30g/1oz) cilantro leaves
½ cup (15g/½oz) Thai basil leaves
¼ cup (30g/1¼oz) raw almonds, chopped
1 teaspoon sesame oil

FOR THE DRESSING

juice of 2 limes
3 tablespoons Paleo-friendly fish sauce
1 tablespoon chili paste
1 teaspoon raw honey
1 teaspoon sesame oil

1. In a large bowl, whisk together the lime juice, coconut aminos, honey, chili paste, garlic, and ginger. Add the flank steak and marinate for 5 minutes.
2. In the meantime, on a large platter, arrange the lettuce, avocado, cucumber, onion, scallions, cilantro, basil, and almonds.
3. Preheat a grill or grill pan over high heat and brush with the sesame oil.
4. Drain the steak and pat dry. Grill the steak about 5 minutes per side for medium rare. Let rest for 5 minutes. Slice against the grain and arrange slices on top of the salad.
5. To make the dressing, whisk together the lime juice, fish sauce, chili paste, honey, and sesame oil in a medium bowl.
6. Pour the dressing over the salad and serve.

CAL 420 | CAL FROM FAT 180 | TOTAL FAT 21G | SAT FAT 4G | SODIUM 700MG | FIBER 6G | PRO 29G

COLESLAW

Generally, coleslaw takes hours to marinate. But with today's hectic schedules, who has the time? This version is ready in less than 30 minutes (although if you want a more intensely developed flavor, you can certainly let it marinate overnight). A handy shortcut? The shredding blade on a food processor makes this coleslaw even easier to prepare.

▶ Preparation Time: 5 minutes | Cooking Time: 0 minutes | Total Time: 5 minutes | SERVES 8

½ large green cabbage, shredded
½ large red cabbage, shredded
2 large carrots, shredded
½ cup (120ml/4fl oz) unfiltered apple cider vinegar
¼ cup (60ml/3fl oz) raw honey
¼ cup (60ml/2fl oz) olive oil
2 tablespoons Whole-Grain Mustard (page 191)
1 tablespoon celery seed
1 teaspoon dry mustard
1 teaspoon sea salt

1. Combine all ingredients in a large bowl and toss to coat.
2. Allow to marinate for 25 minutes, then serve.

CAL 150 | CAL FROM FAT 70 | TOTAL FAT 8G | SAT FAT 1G | SODIUM 300MG | FIBER 4G | PRO 2G

CHAPTER 3

FISH & SEAFOOD

LETTUCE-WRAPPED FISH TACOS WITH TOMATO-PEACH SALSA

I love fish tacos! Marinated tilapia wrapped in lettuce tortillas with a sweet, spicy salsa makes for a deliciously light dinner that is packed with flavor. This is an ideal summer meal when nectarines and tomatoes are at peak season.

▶ Preparation Time: 20 minutes | Cooking Time: 6 minutes | Total Time: 26 minutes | SERVES 4

1 teaspoon olive oil
1 teaspoon ground cumin
1 teaspoon chili powder
juice of 1 lime
½ teaspoon sea salt
4 x 4oz (110g) tilapia fillets, cut in half lengthwise
8 Boston lettuce leaves
½ cup (58g/2oz) radishes, thinly sliced
2 limes, quartered
1 avocado, peeled, pitted, and sliced

FOR THE SALSA

1 peach or nectarine, diced
1 cup (350g/12oz) grape tomatoes, quartered
½ small red onion, diced
¼ cup (15g/½oz) chopped cilantro
juice of 1 lime
1 small jalapeño, seeded and diced
¼ teaspoon sea salt

1. In a large bowl, combine the olive oil, cumin, chili powder, lime juice, and salt and mix well. Add the tilapia and mix to coat. Allow to marinate in the refrigerator for 15 minutes.
2. In the meantime, make the salsa. In a small bowl, combine the peach or nectarine, tomatoes, onion, cilantro, lime juice, jalapeño, and salt and mix well. Set aside.
3. Arrange the lettuce leaves, radishes, limes, and avocado slices on a platter.
4. Heat a large nonstick sauté pan over medium-high heat, then add the marinated tilapia and sear for 3 minutes on each side.
5. Transfer the cooked fish to a platter and serve with the salsa and accompaniments.

CAL 250 | CAL FROM FAT 100 | TOTAL FAT 11G | SAT FAT 2G | SODIUM 380MG | FIBER 6G | PRO 26G

GREEN COCONUT FISH CURRY

Curry is an incredible ingredient with many health benefits, and the Green Curry Paste (page 201) in the Make-Ahead chapter of this book is no exception—it's made with spices and chilies, which help to reduce the risk of mental diseases, boost immunity, ease digestion, and burn fat. You need to make this curry now!

▶ Preparation Time: 16 minutes | Cooking Time: 13–14 minutes | Total Time: 29–30 minutes | SERVES 4

1 tablespoon olive oil
1 jalapeño, seeded and sliced
1 large sweet onion, thinly sliced
1 red bell pepper, thinly sliced
¼ squash or small pumpkin peeled and cut into 1" (2.5cm) pieces
½ cup (50g/2oz) white mushrooms, quartered
2 to 3 tablespoons Green Curry Paste (page 201)

FOR THE SAUCE

1 x 14fl oz (400ml) can coconut milk
¼ cup (60ml/2fl oz) vegetable or fish broth
1 tablespoon Paleo-friendly fish sauce
1 tablespoon raw honey
4 cups (120g/4oz) tatsoi or spinach
1½lbs (675g/24oz) sea bass or red snapper fillets, skinned and cut into 1" (2.5cm) pieces

1. Heat the olive oil in a large, deep sauté pan or wok over high heat until smoking. Add the jalapeño, onion, and bell pepper. Stir-fry for 4–5 minutes, or until lightly browned and the peppers are crisp-tender.
2. Add the pumpkin or squash to the pan and stir-fry for 5 minutes.
3. In the meantime, make the sauce. In a small bowl, mix together the Green Curry Paste, coconut milk, broth, fish sauce, and raw honey.
4. Pour the sauce into the pan, stir, and reduce heat to medium.
5. Add the tatsoi or spinach and stir-fry for another minute or until wilted.
6. Add the fish and cook, stirring occasionally, for 3 minutes, or until flaky.
7. Stir in the basil, then serve.

CAL 320 | CAL FROM FAT 90 | TOTAL FAT 10G | SAT FAT 5G | SODIUM 650MG | FIBER 3G | PRO 37G

PAN-ROASTED STRIPED BASS WITH FENNEL SLAW

This is such an elegant and simple dish. The raw honey forms a caramelized crust on the skin side of the fish that is perfection! With the crunchy texture of the fennel slaw, buttery texture of the fish, and caramelized crust of the fish skin, your mouth is going to be on delicious overload!

▶ Preparation Time: 7 minutes | Cooking Time: 11 minutes | Total Time: 18 minutes | SERVES 4

1 garlic clove, minced
1 thyme sprig, leaves only
1 teaspoon sea salt
1 teaspoon freshly ground black pepper
4 x 4oz (120g) striped bass fillets, skin on
1 teaspoon raw honey
1 tablespoon olive oil

FOR THE SLAW
1 fennel bulb, thinly sliced
1 scallion, thinly sliced
1 tablespoon freshly squeezed orange juice
1 teaspoon olive oil
1 teaspoon unfiltered apple cider vinegar
½ teaspoon sea salt
½ teaspoon freshly ground black pepper

1. Preheat the oven to 400°F. Line a baking sheet with parchment paper.
2. Make the slaw. In a medium bowl, combine the fennel, scallions, orange juice, olive oil, vinegar, salt, and pepper. Mix well and set aside.
3. To prepare the fish, combine the garlic, thyme, salt, and pepper and mix well. Place the fillets on the baking sheet and sprinkle the seasoning over each side. Drizzle with honey.
4. Heat the olive oil in a large non-stick sauté pan over medium-high heat and swirl the oil to coat the entire pan. Add the fillets, skin side down, and pan-fry for 3 minutes, or until a caramelized crust forms on the skin. Do not move the fillets around.
5. Turn once and pan-fry for an additional 3 minutes, or until golden brown and caramelized. Transfer the fish to the baking sheet.
6. Bake the fish in the oven for 5 minutes, or until cooked throughout.
7. Serve immediately with the fennel slaw.

CAL 180 | CAL FROM FAT 70 | TOTAL FAT 7G | SAT FAT 1G | SODIUM 820MG | FIBER 2G | PRO 21G

THAI FISH CAKES WITH CUCUMBER RELISH

Thai flavors in this dish are perfectly harmonious. I enjoy these fish cakes with salmon, but cod also works just as well and tastes great! If you can't find fresh kaffir lime leaves, you can often find kaffir lime leaves in a jar in the Asian section of your grocery store. If you can't find either, you may substitute with an equal amount of lime zest.

▶ Preparation Time: 15 minutes | Cooking Time: 8 minutes | Total Time: 23 minutes | MAKES 12 CAKES

1½lbs (675g/24oz) wild cod or salmon fillets, skin removed and cut into chunks
1 organic free-range egg
3 tablespoons kaffir lime leaves, chopped, or the zest of 1½ limes
1 tablespoon arrowroot
1 tablespoon Paleo-friendly fish sauce
1 tablespoon red curry paste
1 teaspoon raw honey
1 teaspoon sea salt
½ cup (40g/1½oz) snow peas, thinly sliced
2 teaspoons olive oil

FOR THE RELISH

¼ cup (60ml/2fl oz) filtered water
¼ cup (60ml/2fl oz) unfiltered apple cider vinegar
1 tablespoon raw honey
1 teaspoon sea salt
1 cucumber, thinly sliced
1 shallot, thinly sliced
1 jalapeño, thinly sliced

1. To make the cucumber relish, combine the water, vinegar, honey, and salt in a small bowl and mix well. Add the cucumber, shallot, and jalapeño and well mix. Set aside.
2. In a food processor, combine the fish, egg, kaffir lime leaves or lime zest, arrowroot, fish sauce, curry paste, honey, and salt. Pulse 10 times, or until smooth and well combined.
3. Wet your hands and shape the fish mixture into twelve rounded cakes that are 2" (5cm) wide and ½" (1.5cm) high. Insert a small amount of sliced snow peas in the middle of each cake.
4. Heat the olive oil in a large nonstick sauté pan over medium-high heat. Add the fish cakes and fry for about 4 minutes, or until brown. Flip and fry for another 4 minutes, or until brown.
5. Serve fish cakes with the cucumber relish.

CAL 370 | CAL FROM FAT 120 | TOTAL FAT 14G | SAT FAT 3G | SODIUM 1430MG | FIBER 1G | PRO 41G

INDIAN SHRIMP CURRY

This dish features so many ingredients with health benefits. Turmeric has been shown to reduce swelling and ease the pain associated with inflammation of the joints. The capsaicin in chili peppers has been shown to boost the body's immunity and its ability to heal. If one dish can do all of that, then why not enjoy it tonight for dinner?

▶ Preparation Time: 8 minutes | Cooking Time: 15–16 minutes | Total Time: 23–24 minutes | SERVES 4

1lb (450g/16oz) large shrimp, peeled and deveined
½ teaspoon ground turmeric
½ teaspoon sea salt
1 tablespoon olive oil
1 cup (60g/2oz) cilantro, chopped
2 jalapeños, seeded and chopped
2 Roma tomatoes, finely chopped
1 teaspoon cumin seeds
1 teaspoon ground coriander
1 cup (240ml/8fl oz) filtered water

1. In a medium bowl, combine the shrimp, turmeric, and salt and mix well. Marinate in the refrigerator for 5 minutes.
2. Heat the olive oil in a large, deep sauté pan over high heat. Add the shrimp, and stir-fry for 2–3 minutes, or until pink and opaque. Transfer shrimp to a bowl and cover with foil.
3. Using a pestle and mortar, pound the cilantro, garlic, and jalapeños into a fine paste.
4. Add the cilantro paste to the sauté pan and stir-fry for 1 minute, or until fragrant.
5. Add the tomatoes, cumin seeds, and coriander and-stir-fry for another minute.
6. Add the water and mix well. Bring to a boil, then reduce the heat to medium and simmer for 10 minutes.
7. Add the shrimp back into the curry and cook for another 30 seconds. Serve immediately.

CAL 150 | CAL FROM FAT 45 | TOTAL FAT 5G | SAT FAT 1G | SODIUM 1034MG | FIBER 1G | PRO 17G

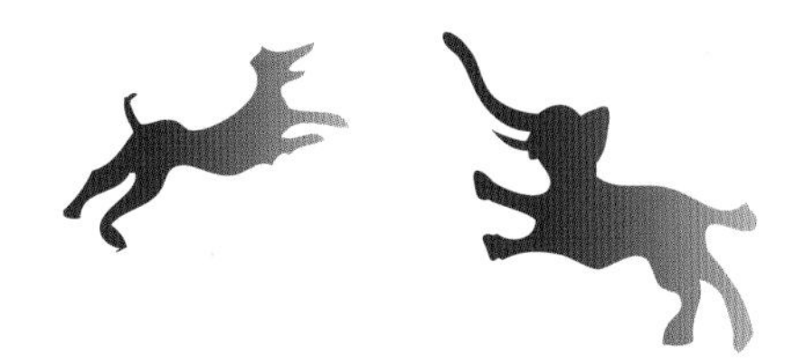

ROSEMARY SHRIMP SKEWERS

This is super simple in preparation, but breathtaking in appearance. When buying the rosemary sprigs—or better yet, cutting them from your own garden—make sure they are at least 6" (15cm) in length.

▶ Preparation Time: 15 minutes | Cooking Time: 6–8 minutes | Total Time: 21–23 minutes | SERVES 4

8 large rosemary sprigs
1lb (450g/16oz) large shrimp, peeled and deveined
3 garlic cloves, minced
zest and juice of 1 large lemon
1 tablespoon olive oil
½ teaspoon sea salt
1 teaspoon freshly ground black pepper

1. To make the skewers, remove the leaves from the bottom three-quarters of each sprig. Chop the leaves and set aside. Reserve the sprigs.
2. In a large bowl, combine the shrimp, garlic, lemon zest and juice, olive oil, and 2 tablespoons chopped rosemary. Mix well, season with salt and pepper, and allow to marinate for 3 minutes.
3. Skewer four shrimp onto each sprig.
4. Heat a large nonstick sauté pan over high heat. Add the skewers and sear for 3–4 minutes on each side, or until bright pink and browned.
5. Serve hot or at room temperature.

CAL 140 | CAL FROM FAT 45 | TOTAL FAT 5G | SAT FAT 0.5G | SODIUM 740MG | FIBER 0G | PRO 20G

SEARED LIME & PEPPER TUNA WITH TROPICAL SALSA

The key to this dish is buying the highest-quality ahi tuna that can be eaten raw. You just need to sear the tuna lightly for the perfect lime-pepper crust and delicious bright-red center. The salsa is wonderful! You will be looking to add it to loads of other recipes.

▶ Preparation Time: 20 minutes | Cooking Time: 4–6 minutes | Total Time: 24–26 minutes | SERVES 4

grated zest of 9 limes
4 tablespoons freshly ground black pepper
1 teaspoon sea salt
4 x 6oz (175g) sushi-grade ahi tuna steaks
1 tablespoon olive oil

FOR THE SALSA

1 cup (350g/12oz) mango, diced
1 cup (225g/8oz) pineapple, diced
1 red bell pepper, diced
½ red onion, diced
1 jalapeño, seeded and diced
¾ cup (45g/1½oz) cilantro, chopped
juice of 2 limes
½ teaspoon sea salt

1. Make the salsa. In a medium bowl, combine all the salsa ingredients, mix well, and set aside.
2. On a large plate, combine the lime zest, salt, and pepper. Dredge the tuna steaks in the zest mixture, pressing down on each side.
3. Heat the oil in a large nonstick sauté pan over high heat. Add the tuna steaks and sear for 2–3 minutes on each side for rare. Slice the tuna and serve with the salsa.

CAL 340 | CAL FROM FAT 110 | TOTAL FAT 12G | SAT FAT 2.5G | SODIUM 580MG | FIBER 2G | PRO 40G

ZUCCHINI PASTA WITH SHRIMP, CHORIZO & SAFFRON

This dish is so superb you won't miss the pasta one little bit! The delicious combination of zucchini noodles, saffron, chorizo, and shrimp creates a balanced, Mediterranean-inspired dish. Enjoy!

▶ Preparation Time: 20 minutes | Cooking Time: 8–10 minutes | Total Time: 28–30 minutes | SERVES 6

3 zucchini
½ cup (120ml/4fl oz) dry white wine
¼ cup (60ml/2fl oz) chicken or vegetable broth
1 teaspoon saffron threads
1 teaspoon olive oil
2 links chicken chorizo, cut in half lengthwise and sliced
1 to 2 teaspoons crushed red pepper, depending on desired spiciness
¾lb (340g/12oz) shrimp, peeled and deveined
1 teaspoon chili powder
½ teaspoon sea salt
½ teaspoon freshly ground black pepper
4 garlic cloves, minced
½ cup (20g/¾oz) basil leaves, torn

1. To prepare the zucchini pasta, trim off the top and bottom of the zucchini. Using a mandoline, slice long, thin, julienned pasta-like strips and set aside.
2. In a medium bowl, combine the white wine, broth, and saffron. Set aside.
3. Heat the olive oil in a large non-stick sauté pan over medium-high heat. Add the chorizo and red pepper flakes, then sauté, stirring frequently, for 3–4 minutes, or until browned and cooked through.
4. Add the shrimp, chili powder, salt, and pepper and sauté for 2–3 minutes, or until the shrimp is bright pink.
5. Stir in the wine-broth mixture, zucchini pasta, and garlic, and sauté for 3 minutes, or until the wine has cooked off and the zucchini pasta is tender.
6. Stir in the basil and serve.

CAL 170 | CAL FROM FAT 50 | TOTAL FAT 6G | SAT FAT 1.5G | SODIUM 720MG | FIBER 3G | PROTEIN 15G

BLACK SEA BASS WITH TAHINI & HARISSA-CUMIN SAUCES

This is going to be your new favorite fish dish! It touches every single flavor palate—sweet, spicy, salty, sour—fabulously! Serve this decadent fish with a simple side such as Sautéed Spinach with Garlic & Chili (page 160).

▶ Preparation Time: 25 minutes | Cooking Time: 5 minutes | Total Time: 30 minutes | SERVES 4

½ cup (120ml/4½fl oz) Spicy Harissa Paste (page 188)
1 tablespoon raw honey
1 tablespoon ground cumin
¼ teaspoon sea salt
4 x 7oz (200g) black sea bass fillets
¼ cup (15g/½oz) cilantro leaves, for garnish

FOR THE SAUCES

½ cup (120ml/4fl oz) tahini
¼ cup (60ml/2fl oz) filtered water
juice of 1 lemon
¼ teaspoon cayenne pepper
¾ teaspoon sea salt
¼ cup (60ml/2¼fl oz) Spicy Harissa Paste (page 188)
1 tablespoon raw honey
1 teaspoon ground cumin

1. Preheat the oven to broil and place the grill rack at the top shelf. Line a baking sheet with aluminum foil and set aside.
2. In a large bowl, combine the harissa, honey, cumin, and salt and mix well. Add the black sea bass fillets and marinate in the refrigerator for 20 minutes.
3. In the meantime, make the two sauces. In a small bowl, whisk together the tahini, water, lemon juice, cayenne, and salt until smooth, adding more water if you prefer a thinner consistency. Set aside.
4. In another small bowl, whisk together the harissa, honey, and cumin and set aside. Transfer the marinated fillets to the baking sheet, draining and discarding any remaining marinade. Broil the fish for 3–5 minutes, or until crispy and cooked through.
5. Plate the fish, drizzle the sauces on top, and garnish with cilantro leaves.

CAL 510 | CAL FROM FAT 310 | TOTAL FAT 34G | SAT FAT 3G | SODIUM 1290MG | FIBER 3G | PRO 33G

ROASTED SALMON WITH PANCETTA & SWISS CHARD

This simple dish is beautifully presented, so it's perfectly suited for company. Pre-diced pancetta shaves off a little prep time, but if you are dicing it yourself, use a ¼" (1.5cm)-thick slice of pancetta and dice.

▶ Preparation Time: 7 minutes | Cooking Time: 12–15 minutes | Total Time: 19–22 minutes | SERVES 4

4 x 5oz (140g) wild salmon fillets, skin on
1 teaspoon sea salt, divided
1 teaspoon freshly ground black pepper, divided
½ cup (40g/1½oz) pancetta, diced
2 garlic cloves, minced
½ teaspoon crushed red pepper flakes
1 head red Swiss chard, thinly sliced
2 tablespoons balsamic vinegar
1 tablespoon olive oil

1. Preheat the oven to 425°F.
2. Place the salmon fillets, skin side down, on your work surface. Cut a slit lengthwise down the middle of each fillet, starting ¼" (6mm) from the top and ending ¼" (6mm) from the bottom. Do not pierce the skin. Push the two ends together, creating a pocket in the center. Season the fillets with ½ teaspoon each salt and pepper.
3. In a large sauté pan over medium-high heat, add the pancetta and sauté, stirring occasionally, for 2 minutes, or until browned and crispy.
4. Add the garlic and red pepper flakes and stir for another 10 seconds, or until fragrant.
5. Add the Swiss chard and sauté, stirring occasionally, for another 3 minutes, or until wilted. Season with balsamic vinegar and the remaining salt and pepper.
6. Divide the chard mixture among the four fillets. It's okay if it mounds over the salmon—you aren't going to flip the salmon over, so load it up!
7. Heat the olive oil in the same sauté pan over medium-high heat. Once the oil is hot, add the salmon fillets, skin side down, and pan-fry for 4 minutes, or until a crisp crust forms. Do not move the fish around.
8. Transfer the sauté pan to the oven and cook another 3–5 minutes, depending on how you like the salmon cooked.

CAL 280 | CAL FROM FAT 90 | TOTAL FAT 10G | SAT FAT 2.5G | SODIUM 880MG | FIBER 1G | PRO 41G

JUMBO CRAB CAKES WITH BACON, SPINACH & HONEY-MUSTARD SAUCE

The best crab cake is one that is mainly crab, not filler! Make sure not to overmix the crab mixture to ensure your lump crab stays that way. Serve with a nice salad for a well-rounded meal.

▶ Preparation Time: 7 minutes | Cooking Time: 12–13 minutes | Total Time: 19–20 minutes | MAKES 8 CAKES

¼ cup (60ml/2fl oz) Homemade Mayonnaise (page 187)
¾ cup (75g/2½oz) almond meal, divided
3 scallions, chopped
3 garlic cloves, minced
¼ cup (10g/¼oz) parsley, chopped
½ teaspoon sea salt
¾ teaspoon freshly ground black pepper, divided
⅛ teaspoon cayenne pepper
1lb (450g/16oz) jumbo lump crabmeat, picked over for shells
3 tablespoons bacon fat or olive oil
5 slices bacon, diced
⅔ lb (300g/10½oz) baby spinach
2 tablespoons Simple Mustard (page 191)
2 tablespoons Dijon mustard
2 tablespoons raw honey

1. Preheat the oven to 300°F. Line a baking sheet with paper towels and set aside.
2. In a large bowl, combine the mayonnaise, ¼ cup (25g) almond meal, scallions, garlic, parsley, salt, ½ teaspoon pepper, and cayenne and mix well. Fold in the crabmeat.
3. Shape the crab mixture into eight patties. Coat the patties with the remaining ½ cup (50g) almond meal.
4. Heat the bacon fat or olive oil in a large sauté pan over medium heat. Add the crab cakes, working in batches if necessary, and fry for about 2 minutes, or until golden brown and crisp. Flip and fry for another 2 minutes, or until golden brown. Transfer the crab cakes to the prepared baking sheet and keep warm in the oven. Repeat with the remaining crab cakes, if cooking in batches.
5. Once the crab cakes have been cooked, prepare the bacon in the same sauté pan over medium heat. Cook for about 4–5 minutes, or until crispy and brown. Season with ¼ teaspoon pepper.
6. Add the spinach and cook, stirring frequently, for 2 minutes, or until wilted.
7. To make the honey-mustard sauce, add the Dijon and honey to a small bowl and combine well.
8. To serve, spoon the spinach onto a platter or four individual plates and top with the crab cakes and honey-mustard sauce.

CAL 650 | CAL FROM FAT 410 | TOTAL FAT 46G | SAT FAT 8G | SODIUM 1000MG | FIBER 6G | PRO 39G

BLACKENED HALIBUT WITH MANGO SALSA

Spicy blackened halibut with a cool and refreshing mango salsa is an inspired alternative to midweek meals. This dish is so simple and flavorful, all it needs is some grilled or sautéed veggies to round out a perfectly balanced meal.

▶ Preparation Time: 15 minutes | Cooking Time: 11–13 minutes | Total Time: 26–28 minutes | SERVES 4

4 x 6oz (175g) halibut fillets, skin on
2 tablespoons olive oil
1 tablespoon garlic powder
1 teaspoon smoked paprika
1 teaspoon chili powder
1 teaspoon dried oregano
1 teaspoon dried thyme
1 teaspoon sea salt
1 teaspoon freshly ground black pepper

FOR THE SALSA
1 large mango, diced
1 jalapeño, seeded and diced
½ red onion, diced
½ red bell pepper, diced
¼ cup (15g/½oz) cilantro, chopped
juice of 2 limes
¼ teaspoon sea salt

1. Preheat the oven to 400°F.
2. In a medium bowl, combine all the ingredients for the salsa and mix well. Set aside.
3. In a large bowl, combine the fish, olive oil, and spices and mix well until fish is evenly coated.
4. Heat a large nonstick, ovenproof sauté pan over medium heat. Once the pan is hot, add the fish fillets skin side down. Cook for 3 minutes, flip, and cook for another 3 minutes.
5. Transfer the pan to the preheated oven and cook 5–7 minutes, or until the fish is cooked through and flaky.
6. To serve, top each fillet with the salsa. Enjoy!

CAL 290 | CAL FROM FAT 90 | TOTAL FAT 10G | SAT FAT 1.5G | SODIUM 750MG | FIBER 2G | PRO 33G

SIMPLE FISHERMAN'S STEW

Bouillabaisse, cioppino—whatever you wish to call this dish, it's so unbelievably satisfying! Although it does have a lot of ingredients, the stew comes together quickly so the extra effort is worth it. When cleaning the mussels and clams, make sure you discard any ones that do not close when pressure is put upon the valve.

▶ Preparation Time: 8 minutes | Cooking Time: 15–16 minutes | Total Time: 23–24 minutes | SERVES 6

¼ cup (60ml/2fl oz) olive oil
1 fennel head, fronds removed and reserved, bulb thinly shaved
1 sweet onion, thinly sliced
1 x 28oz (800g) can diced Italian tomatoes
6 garlic cloves, minced
½ tablespoon crushed red pepper flakes
1 teaspoon saffron threads
1 cup (240ml/8fl oz) dry white wine
2 quarts, or 8 cups, (1.9l/64fl oz) fish stock
1lb (450g/16oz) fresh baby clams, scrubbed and rinsed clean
2lbs (900g/32oz) fresh mussels, scrubbed and rinsed clean
1lb (450g/16oz) firm, skinless fish fillets (such as grouper, snapper, or swordfish), cut into 1" (2.5cm) pieces
1lb (450g/16oz) shrimp, peeled and deveined
1 teaspoon sea salt
¼ cup (10g/⅓ oz) chopped basil, to garnish

1. Heat the olive oil in a large stockpot over medium heat. Add the fennel bulb and onion and sauté for 3 minutes. Add the tomatoes, garlic, red pepper flakes, saffron, and white wine and simmer for 5 minutes.
2. Add the fish stock and bring to a boil.
3. Reduce the heat to medium and add the clams. Cover and steam for 2 minutes, or until they begin to open.
4. Add the mussels and fish, cover, and steam for another 2 minutes.
5. Add the shrimp and cook, uncovered, for another 3–4 minutes, or until the clams and mussels open, the fish is cooked through, and the shrimp are bright pink.
6. Season with the salt.
7. To serve, ladle into bowls and garnish with fresh basil, and fennel fronds.

CAL 580 | CAL FROM FAT 190 | TOTAL FAT 21G | SAT FAT 4G | SODIUM 1000MG | FIBER 3G | PRO 62G

SPICY THAI TUNA BURGERS WITH LIME-GINGER DIPPING SAUCE

This fish burger comes together in no time! Serve with the Spicy Baked Sweet Potato Fries (page 155) or Carrot Fries with Avocado Aioli (page 150) and the meal is complete. To cut down on the time, chop up the ginger, garlic, cilantro, and jalapeño for the burgers and sauce at the same time. The key to this delicious tuna burger is sushi-grade ahi tuna.

▶ Preparation Time: 7 minutes | Cooking Time: 2–4 minutes | Total Time: 9–11 minutes | SERVES 4

- 1½lbs (675g/24oz) sushi-grade ahi tuna, cut into large chunks
- ¼ red onion, minced
- ½ jalapeño, seeded and minced
- 2 tablespoons chopped cilantro
- 2 tablespoons Homemade Mayonnaise (page 187)
- 1 tablespoon coconut aminos
- 1 tablespoon toasted sesame seeds
- 1 teaspoon fresh ginger root, peeled and minced
- 1 garlic clove, minced
- 2 teaspoons sesame oil
- 8 butter lettuce leaves

FOR THE SAUCE

- juice of 1 lime
- 2 tablespoons Paleo-friendly fish sauce
- 1 tablespoon raw honey
- 2 teaspoons unfiltered apple cider vinegar
- 1 teaspoon sesame oil
- 1 teaspoon cilantro, chopped
- 1 garlic clove, minced
- ¼ jalapeño, seeded and minced

1. In a food processor, add the fresh tuna. Pulse 5 times, or until the tuna is finely diced but not overprocessed.
2. In a large bowl, combine the tuna, onion, jalapeño, cilantro, mayonnaise, coconut aminos, sesame seeds, ginger, and garlic and mix well. Shape into four patties.
3. Heat the sesame oil in a large sauté pan over high heat. Add the tuna burgers and sear for 1–2 minutes, depending on your preferred doneness, then flip and sear for another 1–2 minutes.
4. In the meantime, make the sauce. In a medium bowl, whisk together all the ingredients.
5. To serve, place a tuna burger between two lettuce leaves and serve with the sauce.

CAL 580 | CAL FROM FAT 120 | TOTAL FAT 13G | SAT FAT 2.5G | SODIUM 800MG | FIBER 1G | PRO 41G

CHAPTER 4

PORK, LAMB & BEEF

SPICY MINI MEATLOAVES

Meatloaf has never been this simple or delicious. If you don't like your meatloaf super spicy, lower the amount of crushed red pepper. These would be wonderful served with a simple salad and the Roasted Garlic Mashed Cauliflower (page 156).

▶ Preparation Time: 7 minutes | Cooking Time: 15–17 minutes | Total Time: 22–24 minutes | SERVES 6

olive oil for greasing
1½lbs (680g/24oz) organic grass-fed ground beef
1 organic free-range egg
½ sweet onion, finely diced
4 garlic cloves, minced
2 tablespoons nutritional yeast
1 tablespoon Italian seasoning
½ tablespoon crushed red pepper flakes
½ tablespoon fennel seeds
1 teaspoon sea salt
1 teaspoon freshly ground black pepper

FOR THE SAUCE

½ cup tomato paste (120ml/4½fl oz)
2 tablespoons Simple Mustard (page 191)
1 tablespoon raw honey
1 tablespoon Worcestershire Sauce (page 186)
1 teaspoon Hot Pepper Sauce (page 197)
¼ teaspoon sea salt
¼ teaspoon freshly ground black pepper

1. Preheat the oven to 425°F. Grease a 12-cup muffin tin with olive oil.
2. In a large bowl, add the ground beef, egg, onion, garlic, yeast, Italian seasoning, red pepper flakes, fennel seeds, salt, and pepper and mix well.
3. Divide the mixture into twelve equal portions and place in the prepared muffin tin. Bake for 10 minutes.
4. In the meantime, make the sauce. In a small bowl, combine all the ingredients and mix well.
5. Remove the tin from the oven and brush the meatloaves with the prepared sauce.
6. Transfer the meatloaves back to the oven and bake for an additional 5–7 minutes, or until cooked through. Serve immediately.

CAL 290 | CAL FROM FAT 140 | TOTAL FAT 16G | SAT FAT 6G | SODIUM 610MG | FIBER 3G | PRO 26G

FENNEL, SAUSAGE & BASIL PIZZA

This recipe makes two small round pies or one large rectangular pie. The cashews may be replaced with almond meal in the recipe for Pizza Dough (page 182), but I prefer the ground cashews, as it makes for a slightly less sweet dough. The crust will turn out very thin and crispy, and even without the nut cheese, it's a lovely pizza.

▶ Preparation Time: 11 minutes | Cooking Time: 8–11 minutes | Total Time: 19–22 minutes | SERVES 4

Pizza Dough (page 182)
⅓ cup (80ml/2¾fl oz) Pizza Sauce (page 183)
½ cup (125g/4oz) spicy Italian sausage, removed from casing, cooked, and crumbled
¼ fennel bulb, shaved
¼ cup (10g/⅓oz) basil leaves, torn
¼ cup (25g/1oz) nut cheese, crumbled (optional)

1. Follow steps 1–6 in the instructions for making Pizza Dough (page 182).
2. Remove the cooked dough from the oven and increase the temperature to broil. Top with Pizza Sauce, sausage, fennel, basil, and nut cheese, if using.
3. Return the pan(s) to the oven and broil for 1–2 minutes, or until the toppings are crispy and the "cheese" has melted.
4. Remove from the oven, slice, and serve.

CAL 650 | CAL FROM FAT 470 | TOTAL FAT 52G | SAT FAT 9G | SODIUM 1000MG | FIBER 5G | PRO 27G

LAMB & ESCAROLE–STUFFED BAKED PEPPERS

The bold combination of lamb, cinnamon, escarole, and raisins makes this dish so complex and tasty! If you're not a fan of lamb, it can be replaced with ground beef, buffalo, venison, or even turkey. Serve with a simple salad for a unique and elegant meal.

▶ Preparation Time: 15 minutes | Cooking Time: 15 minutes | Total Time: 30 minutes | SERVES 6

3 orange, red, or yellow bell peppers, halved lengthwise, seeded, and membranes removed
1 tablespoon olive oil
1 sweet onion, diced
2 celery ribs, diced
2 carrots, diced
2 garlic cloves, minced
¼ teaspoon ground cinnamon
½ teaspoon dried thyme
1lb (450g/16oz) organic grass-fed ground lamb
½ cup (120ml/4fl oz) tomato puree
½ cup (120ml/4fl oz) chicken broth
2 cups (100g/3½oz) escarole, chopped
½ teaspoon sea salt
½ teaspoon freshly ground black pepper
¼ cup (40g/1½oz) golden raisins
¼ cup (35g/1oz) pine nuts, toasted

1. Preheat the oven to 425°F.
2. Place the pepper halves in a 9" x 11" (23cm x 28cm) glass baking dish. Bake for 15 minutes.
3. In the meantime, prepare the filling. Heat the olive oil in a large nonstick sauté pan over medium heat. Add the onion, celery, and carrots and sauté for 3–5 minutes, or until tender. Add the garlic and stir for 30 seconds.
4. Add the cinnamon and thyme, stir, and cook for another 30 seconds, or until fragrant.
5. Add the lamb and cook for 5 minutes, stirring occasionally and breaking up the lamb as it cooks.
6. Add the tomato puree, chicken broth, and escarole and simmer for 2 minutes, stirring occasionally.
7. Season with salt and pepper. Stir in the raisins and pine nuts.
8. Remove the peppers from the oven and stuff with the lamb filling.
9. Place the dish back into the oven and cook, uncovered, for 15 minutes, or until peppers are tender and stuffing is bubbly and slightly browned. Enjoy!

CAL 310 | CAL FROM FAT 160 | TOTAL FAT 18G | SAT FAT 7G | SODIUM 440MG | FIBER 4G | PRO 21G

PAN-SEARED LAMB CHOPS WITH POMEGRANATE GLAZE

Pomegranate molasses can be found in the international aisle of most grocery stores nowadays and definitely can be ordered online. Combining the flavor of that molasses with the cinnamon and lamb creates a rich, satisfying dish! It reminds me of the holiday season and makes a festive meal when paired with a side that can hold up to the flavors, like Roasted Cauliflower & Pomegranate with Tahini Sauce (page 139) or Roasted Brussels Sprouts with Pancetta & Garlic (page 151) .

▶ Preparation Time: 7 minutes | Cooking Time: 13–17 minutes | Total Time: 20–24 minutes | SERVES 4

¼ cup (60ml/2fl oz) pomegranate molasses
2 teaspoons ground cinnamon
1 teaspoon sea or kosher salt
1½ teaspoons freshly ground black pepper
8 lamb loin chops, 1½" to 2" (4cm to 5cm) thick
2 tablespoons olive oil
½ pomegranate, seeds only
2 tablespoons chopped chives

1. In a large bowl, combine the pomegranate molasses, cinnamon, salt, and pepper and mix well to form a paste. Rub the paste over the lamb chops and allow to sit at room temperature for 5 minutes.
2. Preheat the oven to 375°F and line a baking sheet with aluminum foil.
3. Heat 1 tablespoon olive oil in a large nonstick sauté pan or grill pan over medium heat. Put four lamb chops into the pan and sear for 2 minutes on each side, or until a crust forms. (The pomegranate molasses has a high sugar content, so be careful not to overcook the chops or the crust will easily burn.) After searing the chops on both sides, transfer to the prepared baking sheet. Wipe the sauté or grill pan clean with a paper towel and repeat with remaining 1 tablespoon oil and four lamb chops.
4. Place the chops in the oven and cook to desired doneness as follows: For rare, bake for 5 minutes, or until internal temperature reaches 120°F. For medium rare, bake approximately 7 minutes, or until internal temperature reaches 130°F. For medium, bake approximately 9 minutes, or until internal temperature reaches 140°F.
5. Once the lamb chops are cooked to the desired doneness, transfer them to a platter, garnish with pomegranate seeds and chives, and serve!

CAL 310 | CAL FROM FAT 80 | TOTAL FAT 9G | SAT FAT 2.5G | SODIUM 550MG | FIBER 1G | PRO 23G

SPICY PORK & VEGETABLE STIR-FRY

A stir-fry is a great way to use up leftover veggies on a night when you need a quick and easy dinner. This one has Chinese long beans, but if you can't find them at your local grocer, green beans, broccoli, bok choy, or even a combination of these would suffice for replacement.

▶ Preparation Time: 15 minutes | Cooking Time: 8–10 minutes | Total Time: 23–25 minutes | SERVES 4

1 tablespoon dry sherry
2 teaspoons tapioca flour
3 tablespoons coconut aminos, divided
2 teaspoons sesame oil
1 x 12oz (350g) organic grass-fed boneless pork loin, thinly sliced and cut into 2" x ¼" (5cm x 6mm) strips
1 teaspoon raw honey
2 teaspoons peanut oil
2 teaspoons fresh ginger root, minced, divided
2 teaspoons garlic, minced, divided
½ teaspoon crushed red pepper flakes, divided
1 red bell pepper, julienned
½lb (225g/8oz) asparagus, cut into 2" (5cm) pieces
1 cup (90g/3oz) Chinese long beans, cut into 2" (5cm) pieces
⅓ broccoli head, florets only
¼ cup (40g/1½oz) roasted salted cashews

1. In a small bowl, combine the sherry, tapioca flour, and 1 tablespoon coconut aminos and mix well. Whisk in the sesame oil.
2. Add the pork, mix well to coat, and let stand for 10 minutes.
3. In a separate small bowl make the sauce. Combine the honey and remaining 2 tablespoons coconut aminos. Set aside.
4. Heat 1 teaspoon peanut oil in a wok or large nonstick skillet over high heat until the oil is just smoking. Add 1 teaspoon ginger, 1 teaspoon garlic, and ¼ teaspoon red pepper flakes and cook until fragrant, about 5 seconds. Add the bell pepper and stir-fry 2 minutes.
5. Add the asparagus, Chinese long beans, broccoli, and cashews. Stir-fry for 2 minutes, or until vegetables are crisp-tender. Transfer vegetables to a bowl.
6. Heat the remaining 1 tablespoon peanut oil in the wok or skillet until just smoking. Stir-fry the remaining ginger, garlic, and red pepper flakes until fragrant, about 5 seconds.
7. Add the pork and stir-fry, separating the strips, for 2–3 minutes, or until browned and just cooked through.
8. Return the vegetables to the wok, pour in the honey sauce, and stir-fry for about 1–2 minutes, or until vegetables are al dente.

CAL 250 | CAL FROM FAT 110 | TOTAL FAT 12G | SAT FAT 2.5G | SODIUM 680MG | FIBER 2G | PRO 23G

BEEF & YAM CUTLETS WITH TAHINI SAUCE

This dish is such a warm and comforting one, you should try making it when the temperature drops and your family is craving something filling and delicious! Serve up with a simple side salad for a quick, fuss-free meal.

▶ Preparation Time: 7 minutes | Cooking Time: 16–21 minutes | Total Time: 23–28 minutes | SERVES 4

1 large yam, baked, cooled, and peeled
1 teaspoon sesame oil
1lb (450g/16oz) organic grass-fed ground beef
1 sweet red onion, minced
1 jalapeño or serrano pepper, seeded and minced
1 tablespoon fresh ginger root, minced
4 garlic cloves, minced
1 teaspoon garam masala
1 teaspoon ground cumin
¼ teaspoon turmeric
1 teaspoon sea salt
½ teaspoon freshly ground black pepper
1 organic free-range egg
1 tablespoon olive oil, divided

FOR THE SEASONING
1 cup (100g/3½oz) almond meal
1 teaspoon garam masala
½ teaspoon sea salt
½ teaspoon turmeric
½ teaspoon ground cumin

FOR THE SAUCE
½ cup (120ml/4fl oz) tahini
juice of 2 lemons
½ teaspoon sea salt

1. In a large bowl, mash the yam with a fork or potato masher and set aside.
2. Heat the sesame oil in a large sauté pan over medium-high heat. Add the ground beef, onion, and jalapeño and sauté for 3–4 minutes, or until the beef is browned. Add the ginger, garlic, garam masala, cumin, turmeric, salt, and pepper and sauté for another minute.
3. Add the meat mixture and egg to the mashed yam and mix well.
4. For the seasoning, combine the almond meal, garam masala, salt, turmeric, and cumin on a large plate and mix well.
5. In the same sauté pan, add ½ tablespoon olive oil and heat over medium heat.
6. While oil is heating, form the meat mixture into four patties. Roll each patty in the seasoning.
7. Add half of the patties to the sauté pan and cook 3–4 minutes on each side, or until crispy and browned. Transfer to a paper towel–lined plate and keep warm while you cook the rest of the patties with the remaining ½ tablespoon olive oil.
8. In the meantime, make the sauce. In a medium bowl, combine the tahini, lemon juice, and salt and whisk until combined. Serve patties with the sauce and devour!

CAL 690 | CAL FROM FAT 450 | TOTAL FAT 51G | SAT FAT 10G | SODIUM 1120MG | FIBER 7G | PRO 37G

ADOBO BEEF SLIDERS ON SWEET POTATO "BUNS" WITH BBQ SAUCE & SIMPLE MUSTARD

You can find adobo sauce in the Latin American section of your grocery store. It is traditionally sold in a can as chipotles in adobo sauce. These chilies are potent and spicy and can be added to anything your palate desires. For this recipe, just use the sauce and add as much as you wish to increase or decrease the level of spiciness. If you don't want the sweet potato "bun," a grilled portobello mushroom or Boston lettuce leaves will also work as a delicious vehicle for the burger.

▶ Preparation Time: 5–7 minutes | Cooking Time: 20–23 minutes | Total Time: 25–30 minutes | SERVES 4

2 sweet potatoes, washed and sliced into ¼" (6mm)-thick rounds
1 teaspoon garlic powder
1 teaspoon sweet paprika
1 teaspoon ground cumin
1 teaspoon sea salt, divided
1 tablespoon olive oil
1lb (450g/16oz) organic grass-fed ground beef
1 to 2 tablespoons adobo sauce
2 garlic cloves, minced
2 tablespoons cilantro, chopped
½ teaspoon freshly ground black pepper
8 romaine lettuce leaves
Barbecue Sauce (page 192), to serve
Simple Mustard (page 191), to serve

1. Preheat the oven to 425°F. Line a baking sheet with aluminum foil.
2. In a large bowl, combine the sweet potatoes with the garlic powder, paprika, ½ teaspoon of salt, and olive oil and mix well. Spread potato slices in a single layer on the prepared baking sheet. Bake in the oven for 15–17 minutes.
3. In the meantime, make the burgers. In a medium bowl, combine the ground beef, adobo, garlic, cilantro, remaining ½ teaspoon salt, and pepper and mix well. Form into eight patties.
4. Heat a large skillet or cast-iron grill over medium-high heat. Add the burgers and cook for 3 minutes on each side for medium.
5. To finish the sweet potato "buns," turn the oven to broil and move the potatoes to the top rack. Broil for 1–2 minutes, or until crispy.
6. To serve, place a patty on one side of the sweet potato "bun." Add the Barbeque Sauce, Simple Mustard, and one tomato slice and lettuce leaf, then top with remaining "bun."

CAL 390 | CAL FROM FAT 200 | TOTAL FAT 22G | SAT FAT 7G | SODIUM 1240MG | FIBER 3G | PRO 26G

LETTUCE-WRAPPED SAUSAGE BURGERS

These burgers are always a big hit—a little spicy, a little sweet, and a little amazing! The crunch of the sweet potato chips within the burger is just one of the surprises here. Serve with some Spicy Baked Sweet Potato Fries (page 155) or Carrot Fries with Avocado Aioli (page 150) to satisfy your burger craving.

▶ Preparation Time: 5 minutes | Cooking Time: 9–10 minutes | Total Time: 14–15 minutes | SERVES 4

1lb (450g/16oz) spicy Italian pork sausage meat, casing removed
1 cup (25g/1oz) sweet potato chips, crumbled
1 garlic clove, minced
1 tablespoon Dijon mustard
½ teaspoon sea salt
1 tablespoon duck fat
juice of 1 lime
½ avocado, sliced
8 butter lettuce leaves

FOR THE SAUCE

2 tablespoons raw honey
2 tablespoons Dijon mustard
2 teaspoons yellow mustard

1. Preheat the oven to 400°F.
2. In a medium bowl, combine the sausage meat, sweet potato chips, garlic, Dijon, and salt. Form into four patties.
3. Heat the duck fat in a skillet or grill over high heat.
4. Add the patties and cook for 3 minutes on each side.
5. Drizzle lime juice over the avocado.
6. To make the sauce, in a small bowl, combine the honey and both mustards and mix well. Set aside.
7. Once the burgers form a nice crust on both sides, transfer the skillet or grill to the oven and cook another 3–4 minutes, or until the burgers are cooked through.
8. To serve, make four "buns" with the butter lettuce and place a patty on each "bun." Drizzle with the sauce and add a couple slices of avocado. Enjoy!

CAL 660 | CAL FROM FAT 440 | TOTAL FAT 49G | SAT FAT 15G | SODIUM 1000MG | FIBER 3G | PRO 18G

GREEK MEATBALLS WITH PINE NUTS, GOLDEN RAISINS & TOMATO SAUCE

Do yourself a favor and make these in the summer when tomatoes are in season! Fresh is what counts, so you can use beefsteak tomatoes or other large tomatoes in place of the cherry tomatoes as well. The difference in the sauce is amazing! Meatballs are traditionally slow cooked and time consuming, but these are light, quick, and fresh with the tomato sauce.

▶ Preparation Time: 10–12 minutes | Cooking Time: 15–17 minutes | Total Time: 25–29 minutes
MAKES 32 meatballs | 8 SERVINGS

FOR THE MEATBALLS

1lb (450g/160oz) organic grass-fed ground lamb
1lb (450g/160oz) organic grass-fed ground beef
3 organic free-range eggs
¼ cup (35g/1oz) pine nuts, toasted
¼ cup (40g/1½oz) golden raisins
4 garlic cloves, minced
1 teaspoon dried parsley
1 teaspoon dried oregano
1 teaspoon dried basil
1 teaspoon dried thyme
1 teaspoon ground cinnamon
1 teaspoon sea salt
1 teaspoon freshly ground black pepper

FOR THE SAUCE

3 tablespoons olive oil
1 sweet onion, diced
6 garlic cloves, minced
2 cups (300g/10oz) cherry tomatoes, chopped
¼ cup (10g/⅓oz) basil leaves, chopped
½ teaspoon sea salt
½ teaspoon freshly ground black pepper

1. Preheat the oven to 425°F. Line a baking sheet with aluminum foil.
2. To make the meatballs, combine all the ingredients in a large bowl and mix well to combine.
3. Using a tablespoon scoop and wet hands, form the mixture into balls and place them on the prepared baking sheet.
4. Bake in the oven for 15–17 minutes, or until the meatballs are cooked through.
5. In the meantime, make the sauce. Heat the olive oil in a large sauté pan over medium heat.
6. Add the onion and garlic and sauté for 3–4 minutes, or until translucent and softened.
7. Add the tomatoes, basil, salt, and pepper and cook for 1 minute longer, or just until heated through.
8. Serve the meatballs with the tomato sauce.

CAL 430 | CAL FROM FAT 29 | TOTAL FAT 32G | SAT FAT 11G | SODIUM 470MG | FIBER 2G | PRO 25G

GREEK KEBABS WITH CUCUMBER-OLIVE RELISH

These kebabs are simple and flavorful with the combination of lemon, oregano, olives, and garlic. You can also use skirt or hanger steak instead of flank steak—just make sure you slice it thinly. Serve these with some Babaganoush (page 140) or Zucchini Ribbons with Garlic & Mint (page 143) for a savory weeknight meal.

▶ Preparation Time: 20 minutes | Cooking Time: 4–8 minutes | Total Time: 24–28 minutes | SERVES 4

1lb (450g/16oz) organic grass-fed flank steak, thinly sliced against the grain
12 x 6" (15cm) bamboo skewers, soaked in water for 10 minutes
4 garlic cloves, minced
grated zest and juice of 1 lemon
¼ cup (60ml/2fl oz) olive oil
1 tablespoon oregano, chopped
1 teaspoon sea salt
1 teaspoon freshly ground black pepper

FOR THE RELISH

1 English cucumber, ends removed and roughly chopped
½ cup (50g/2oz) pitted kalamata olives
1 tablespoon oregano, leaves

1. Heat a grill or grill pan over high heat.
2. Skewer the sliced beef onto the soaked bamboo skewers. Arrange the skewers in a glass dish with the ends of skewers facing out so that the marinade can be poured over the meat.
3. In a small bowl, whisk together the garlic, lemon zest and juice, olive oil, oregano, salt, and pepper. Pour the marinade over the skewers and allow to marinate at room temperature for 15 minutes.
4. In the meantime, make the relish. In a food processor, combine all the ingredients and pulse about 10–15 times, or until the relish is finely chopped. Transfer to a small bowl.
5. To grill the kebabs, drain the marinade from the skewers and grill for 2–4 minutes on each side, or until charred and cooked to your desired doneness.
6. Serve the skewers with the relish.

CAL 320 | CAL FROM FAT 200 | TOTAL FAT 22G | SAT FAT 4.5G | SODIUM 670MG | FIBER 1G | PRO 26G

QUICK ITALIAN MEATBALLS WITH SPAGHETTI SQUASH "PASTA"

Spaghetti and meatballs is a classic favorite steeped in Italian tradition. In this Paleo-friendly recipe, he meatballs are juicy and tender and the spaghetti squash is packed with flavor without all the gluten. It's an easy mid-week meal that's sure to be enjoyed by adults and kids alike.

▶ Preparation Time: 5 minutes | Cooking Time: 25 minutes | Total Time: 30 minutes | MAKES 16 MEATBALLS

1 spaghetti squash
1lb (450g/16oz) organic grass-fed ground beef
2 organic free-range eggs, lightly beaten
½ cup (50g/1¾oz) almond meal
2 garlic cloves, minced
1 tablespoon Italian seasoning
1½ teaspoons sea salt, divided
1½ teaspoons freshly ground black pepper, divided
olive oil spray
2 cups (485ml/18fl oz) Homemade Marinara (page 185)
2 tablespoons olive oil
¼ cup (10g /⅓oz) basil, chopped

1. Preheat the oven to 450°F. Line two baking sheets with aluminum foil or parchment paper. Pierce the squash all over with a sharp knife and place it on one of the prepared baking sheets. Roast in the oven for 13 minutes, then rotate the sqush halfway and roast for another 12–14 minutes, or until tender.
2. In the meantime, make the meatballs. In a large bowl, combine the ground beef, eggs, almond meal, garlic, Italian seasoning, and 1 teaspoon each salt and pepper. Mix until just combined. Scoop up 2 tablespoons meat mixture and, using wet hands, form into a ball. Repeat for remaining meatballs. Place the meatballs on the second prepared baking sheet, spray with olive oil spray, and bake for 10 minutes.
3. Warm the Homemade Marinara in a medium saucepan over medium heat. Once the meatballs are cooked, add them into sauce and continue to cook for 5 minutes.
4. Remove the squash from the oven and cut it in half lengthwise. Remove the seeds and discard. Using a fork, scoop the flesh of the squash into a large bowl. Add the olive oil, basil, and remaining ½ teaspoon each salt and pepper to the bowl and stir to combine.
5. To serve, plate the spaghetti squash and then top with the sauce and meatballs.

CAL 480 | CAL FROM FAT 300 | TOTAL FAT 33G | SAT FAT 9G | SODIUM 880MG | FIBER 5G | PRO 31G

GRILLED LAMB BURGERS WITH A FRIED EGG OVER SAUTÉED GREENS

If you're short on inspiration and time, look no further than this yummy treat. A perfectly fried egg over grass-fed lamb is accented here with the spicy flavors of vibrant winter greens. . .it's delicious! What impresses even more than the taste is the fact that it can be prepared under 20 minutes.

▶ Preparation Time: 5 minutes | Cooking Time: 13–18 minutes | Total Time: 18–23 minutes | SERVES 4

2 tablespoons olive oil, divided
2 garlic cloves, minced
1lb (450g/16oz) mixed winter greens (such as mustard, Tuscan kale, curly kale or collard greens), trimmed
¼ cup (60ml/2fl oz) chicken broth
1½ teaspoons sea salt, divided
2½ teaspoons freshly ground black pepper, divided
2 tablespoons balsamic vinegar
1lb (450g/16oz) organic grass-fed ground lamb
3 garlic cloves, minced
1 tablespoon Dijon mustard
2 tablespoons parsley, chopped
4 organic free-range eggs

1. Preheat a grill or grill pan over medium-high heat.
2. In a large, deep stock pot, heat 1 tablespoon olive oil over medium heat. Add the 2 cloves minced garlic and stir until fragrant, about 20 seconds.
3. Add the winter greens, chicken broth, ½ teaspoon salt, and 1 teaspoon pepper and sauté for 5 minutes, or until wilted. Add the vinegar and set aside. Keep warm.
4. To make the burgers, combine the ground lamb, 3 cloves minced garlic, Dijon, parsley, ½ teaspoon salt, and 1 teaspoon pepper in a medium bowl and mix well. Form into four patties.
5. Once the grill is hot, add the lamb burgers and cook for 3–5 minutes per side, or to desired doneness.
6. Heat remaining 1 tablespoon olive oil in a large nonstick sauté pan over medium heat.
7. Add the four eggs and season with remaining ½ teaspoon each salt and pepper. Cook for 2–3 minutes, or until the egg white is no longer translucent and the yolk is cooked to your desired consistency.
8. To serve, arrange the wilted greens on four plates, top with burgers, and then fried eggs. Enjoy!

CAL 530 | CAL FROM FAT 310 | TOTAL FAT 35G | SAT FAT 12G | SODIUM 1080MG | FIBER 2G | PRO 38G

BACON-MUSTARD-WRAPPED PORK TENDERLOIN WITH SAUTÉED APPLES

This is heart-warming comfort food at its best. The classic flavor combination teams up rich pork and bacon with sharp mustard and sweet, acidic apples. This elegant dish can be served with Rosemary Garlic Spaghetti Squash Fritters (page 161) and a simple salad for a meal made to impress.

▶ Preparation Time: 7 minutes | Cooking Time: 23 minutes | Total Time: 30 minutes | SERVES 4

1 x 1lb (450g/16oz) organic grass-fed boneless pork tenderloin, silver skin removed
2 tablespoons Whole-Grain Mustard (page191)
1 teaspoon sea salt
1 teaspoon freshly ground black pepper
6 slices bacon
kitchen twine
2 Honeycrisp or your favorite apples, cored and diced

1. Preheat the oven to 400°F. Line a baking sheet with aluminum foil and place a rack on top.
2. Rub the tenderloin with the mustard, salt, and pepper. Wrap the strips of bacon over the length of the tenderloin, overlapping slightly. Then wrap the tenderloin with kitchen twine to secure the bacon.
3. Heat a large skillet over high heat. Place the bacon-wrapped tenderloin in the hot pan and sear for 2 minutes per side, turning a total of three times to sear all sides. The tenderloin should be browned on all sides. Do not discard the bacon fat—you will use it to sauté the apples.
4. Transfer the seared tenderloin to the prepared baking sheet, place on the top rack in the oven, and roast for 10 minutes.
5. Transfer the pork to a cutting board, cover with aluminum foil, and allow to rest for 5 minutes.
6. In the meantime, prepare the sautéed apples. In the same skillet you used to sear the pork, heat the reserved bacon fat over medium heat. Add the apples and sauté for 3–4 minutes, or until crisp-tender and lightly browned.
7. Once the pork has rested, remove the twine, slice it into eight pieces, and serve with the sautéed apples.

CAL 320 | CAL FROM FAT 160 | TOTAL FAT 18G | SAT FAT 6G | SODIUM 830MG | FIBER 2G | PRO 28G

ROSEMARY & GARLIC LAMB CHOPS WITH OLIVE SALSA

This understated dish is made of simple ingredients that are packed with flavor. It could happily stand on its own as a one-dish meal, but if you're looking for a stand-out Sunday dinner, it pairs beautifully alongside the Zucchini Ribbons with Garlic & Mint (page 143) or Roasted Broccoli with Pine Nut–Parsley Pesto (page 38). The options are endless!

▶ Preparation Time: 12 minutes | Cooking Time: 4–6 minutes | Total Time: 16–18 minutes | SERVES 4

6 garlic cloves
4 tablespoons rosemary, chopped
3 tablespoons plus 1 teaspoon olive oil
1½ teaspoons sea salt
1½ teaspoons freshly ground black pepper
12 x 2½oz (70g) organic grass-fed lamb rib chops

FOR THE SALSA

1 cup (100g/4oz)) pitted green olives
1 cup (100g/4oz) pitted black olives
1 yellow bell pepper, diced
¼ cup (35g/1oz) pine nuts, toasted
1 tablespoon red wine vinegar

1. Preheat a grill or grill pan over high heat.
2. In a food processor, combine the garlic, rosemary, 3 tablespoons olive oil, salt, and pepper and process for about 30 seconds, or until finely chopped.
3. Transfer to a large bowl, then rub the garlic mixture over the lamb chops and set aside to marinate.
4. In the meantime, make the olive salsa. Add the green and black olives to the food processor and pulse 5–10 times, or until the olives are chopped.
5. In a medium bowl, combine the chopped olives, bell pepper, pine nuts, red wine vinegar and remaining 1 teaspoon olive oil. Allow to marinate while you grill the lamb.
6. Transfer the lamb chops to the preheated grill or grill pan and cook for 2–3 minutes per side for medium rare. Increase the cooking time on each side depending on your preferred doneness.
7. To serve, arrange the lamb chops on a platter and top with the olive salsa.

CAL 600 | CAL FROM FAT 370 | TOTAL FAT 41G | SAT FAT 10G | SODIUM 1200MG | FIBER 2G | PRO 47G

LAMB & VEGETABLE KEBABS WITH MINT-JALAPEÑO CHUTNEY

Kebabs are a summer staple: They come together quickly, and they're definitely crowd-pleasers. Chef's tip: Keep the lamb and vegetables on separate skewers so the vegetables have an opportunity to cook all the way through. The chutney here is also irresistibly good.

▶ Preparation Time: 4 minutes | Cooking Time: 20–24 minutes | Total Time: 24 –28 minutes | SERVES 4

8 x 8" (20cm) wooden skewers, soaked in water for 10 minutes
1½lbs (675g/24oz) organic grass-fed boneless lamb leg, trimmed and cut into 1½" (3.5cm) pieces
2 red, orange, or yellow bell peppers, seeded and cut into 2" (5cm) pieces
1 red onion, cut into 8 wedges
8 crimini mushrooms
2 tablespoons olive oil
juice of 1 lemon
1 tablespoon ground cumin
2½ teaspoons sea salt, divided
1 teaspoon freshly ground black pepper

FOR THE CHUTNEY

2 jalapeños
2 cups (80g/3oz) mint leaves
1 garlic clove
1 tablespoon raw honey
2 tablespoons unfiltered apple cider vinegar

1. Preheat a grill to medium-high heat.
2. In a large bowl, place the lamb. In a separate large bowl, add the peppers, onion (being careful not to break up the wedges), and mushrooms.
3. In a small bowl, combine the olive oil, lemon juice, cumin, 2 teaspoons salt, and pepper. Divide the marinade between the lamb and vegetables and toss to coat.
4. Thread the lamb onto four skewers and set aside on a plate. Thread the vegetables onto the remaining four skewers and set aside on another plate.

5. On the preheated grill, add the jalapeños and grill for 2 minutes. Turn and grill for another 2 minutes, or until charred.
6. Add the vegetable skewers to the grill and cook for 5–6 minutes on each side, or until tender.
7. About 2–3 minutes into grilling the vegetables, add the lamb skewers to the grill. Cook for 8–10 minutes total, turning occasionally, until the lamb reaches desired degree of doneness.
8. To make the chutney, trim off the stems of the jalapeños. In a food processor, add the jalapeños, mint, garlic, honey, vinegar, and remaining ½ teaspoon salt. Process for 1 minute, or until finely chopped and well combined.
9. To serve, arrange the lamb and vegetable kebabs on a platter and drizzle with the chutney.

CAL 340 | CAL FROM FAT 130 | TOTAL FAT 14G | SAT FAT 3.5G | SODIUM 1380MG | FIBER 2G | PRO 37G

CHAPTER 5

POULTRY

CHICKEN LAAB WITH MINT & THAI BASIL IN LETTUCE CUPS

Laab is a light and flavorful Thai dish, and even though it traditionally contains toasted ground rice, this Paleo-friendly version will not disappoint. Serve with Crab, Green Mango, Cucumber & Coconut Salad with Chili Lime Dressing (page 47) or Baby Bok Choy with Ginger & Sesame (page 145) for a light and lovely lunch or dinner.

▶ Preparation Time: 15 minutes | Cooking Time: 8 minutes | Total Time: 23 minutes | SERVES 4

juice of 2 large limes
1lb (450g/16oz) organic free-range ground chicken or turkey, half white meat and half dark meat
1 teaspoon toasted sesame oil
2 shallots, thinly sliced
½ teaspoon crushed red pepper flakes
¼ cup (60ml/fl 2oz) Paleo-friendly fish sauce
2 tablespoons cilantro, chopped
2 tablespoons Thai basil, chopped
2 tablespoons mint, chopped
2 scallions, chopped
2 limes, quartered, to serve
1 head iceberg lettuce, leaves separated and kept whole

1. In a medium bowl, combine the lime juice and ground meat and mix well. Set aside.
2. Heat the sesame oil in a large nonstick sauté pan or wok over medium-high heat. Add the shallots and cook about 3 minutes, or until lightly browned.
3. Add the marinated meat and red pepper flakes and cook, stirring occasionally, for 5 minutes, or until the meat is crumbled and cooked through.
4. Remove from heat, then stir in the fish sauce, cilantro, Thai basil, mint, and scallions. Transfer to a serving dish.
5. To serve, arrange the lettuce leaves and lime wedges on a platter to accompany the laab. Diners can make their own laab lettuce wraps and season with lime juice as desired.

CAL 230 | CAL FROM FAT 100 | TOTAL FAT 11G | SAT FAT 3G | SODIUM 1000MG | FIBER 1G | PRO 22G

WHITE CHICKEN CHILI

Chicken chili is a great alternative to a traditional beef or game chili, but the ingredient that makes this recipe special is the coconut base. Spice-lovers, feel free to add more chili powder or try cayenne powder instead. If you prefer your dishes with a little less heat, then simply reduce the spice. This chili is perfect on a cold winter day.

▶ Preparation Time: 10 minutes | Cooking Time: 21–22 minutes | Total Time: 31–32 minutes | SERVES 4

½ tablespoon olive oil
1lb (450g/16oz) organic free-range ground chicken, white and dark meat
2 tablespoons garlic, minced
2 tablespoons chili powder
1 tablespoon ground cumin
1 teaspoon dried oregano
¼ to 1 teaspoon cayenne pepper
1 teaspoon sea salt
3 bell peppers, diced
2 small sweet onions, diced
1 jalapeño, seeded and diced
1½ cups (350ml/12fl oz) chicken broth
1 x 4oz (113g) can diced green chilies
½ cup (120ml/4fl oz) coconut milk
juice of 2 large limes

FOR THE TOPPING

½ sweet onion, diced
½ cup (30g/1oz) cilantro chopped
2 tablespoons jalapeño, diced

1. Heat the olive oil in a large saucepan over medium-high heat. Add the ground chicken and cook for 3–4 minutes, or until browned and cooked through.
2. Add the garlic, chili powder, cumin, oregano, cayenne, and salt and stir.
3. Add the bell peppers, onions, and jalapeño and sauté for 3 minutes, stirring occasionally.
4. Add the chicken broth and green chilies. Bring to a boil, then reduce the heat to medium and simmer for 15 minutes, or until thickened.
5. In the meantime, make the topping. In a small bowl, add the onion, cilantro, and jalapeño, and mix well. Set aside.
6. Once the chili has finished cooking, remove from heat and add the coconut milk and lime juice. Stir.
7. To serve, ladle into bowls and serve with the topping.

CAL 300 | CAL FROM FAT 160 | TOTAL FAT 18 G | SAT FAT 18G | SODIUM 950MG | FIBER 2G | PRO 23G

ALMOND-CRUSTED CHICKEN TENDERS

These crowd-pleasing chicken tenders are sure to delight every member of the family! Generously seasoned, they taste delicious on their own, but they are irresistible with homemade dipping sauces like Simple Mustard (page 191) or Homemade Ketchup (page 200).

▶ Preparation Time: 8 minutes | Cooking Time: 20–22 minutes | Total Time: 28–30 minutes | SERVES 4

1lb (450g/16oz) organic free-range skinless chicken breasts, trimmed and cut into 2" (5cm) strips
1 cup (100g/3½oz) almond meal
1 tablespoon smoked paprika
1 teaspoon garlic powder
1 teaspoon onion powder
1 teaspoon ground cumin
1 teaspoon sea salt
1 teaspoon freshly ground black pepper
2 organic free-range eggs
olive oil spray
Homemade Ketchup (page 200), to serve
Simple Mustard (page 191), to serve

1. Preheat the oven to 400°F. Line a baking sheet with aluminum foil and place a baking rack on the top shelf of the oven.
2. On a large plate, combine the almond meal, paprika, garlic powder, onion powder, cumin, salt, and pepper and mix well. Set aside.
3. In a shallow bowl, whisk the eggs until frothy.
4. Dredge each chicken strip in the egg wash and then in the almond meal mixture and place each almond-coated chicken tender onto the prepared baking sheet.
5. Spray tenders with olive oil spray on both sides.
6. Bake for 10 minutes, flip, and bake for 10–12 minutes longer.
7. Serve with your favorite dipping sauce.

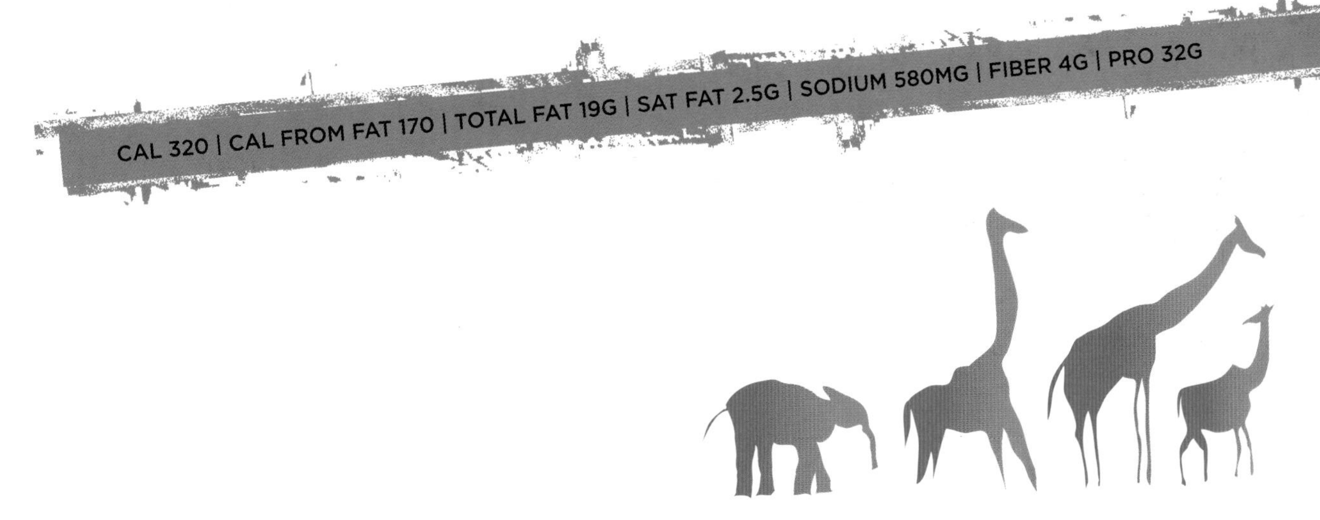

ALMOND-CRUSTED TURKEY CUTLETS WITH TOMATO ARUGULA SALAD

The almonds add texture and flavor to ordinary turkey cutlets here, and they are equally delicious on chicken cutlets. The peppery arugula and tomato make a fitting side dish for this quick and easy meal. I recommend trying it during the summer months when tomatoes and arugula are at their best.

▶ Preparation Time: 5 minutes | Cooking Time: 8–12 minutes | Total Time: 13–17 minutes | SERVES 4

1 cup (100g/3½ oz) almond meal
2 tablespoons Italian seasoning
1 tablespoon crushed red pepper flakes
½ teaspoon sea salt
½ teaspoon freshly ground black pepper
2 organic free-range eggs
8 x 3oz (85g) organic free-range turkey cutlets, thinly pounded
2 tablespoons olive oil, divided
4 cups (80g/3oz) wild arugula
2 cups (300g/10½oz) grape tomatoes, halved lengthwise
¼ teaspoon sea salt
½ teaspoon freshly ground black pepper
1 teaspoon balsamic vinegar

1. On a large plate, combine the almond meal, Italian seasoning, red pepper flakes, salt, and pepper and stir to combine.
2. In a shallow bowl, whisk the eggs until frothy.
3. Dredge the cutlets in the egg wash and then in the almond-meal mixture, coating the cutlets evenly. Set aside.
4. Heat 1 tablespoon olive oil in a large sauté pan over medium-high heat. Add four cutlets and cook 2–3 minutes on each side, or until lightly browned and crispy. Transfer the cutlets to a platter and keep warm. Repeat with the remaining olive oil and cutlets.
5. To make the salad topping, combine the arugula, tomatoes, salt, and pepper in a large bowl.
6. To serve, top the cutlets with the salad and drizzle with balsamic.

CAL 460 | CAL FROM FAT 220 | TOTAL FAT 24G | SAT FAT 3G | SODIUM 690MG | FIBER 4G | PRO 52G

GRILLED HERITAGE CHICKEN WITH SPICY CHIMICHURRI

This dish may be simple, but its flavors are rich and fiery. The chimichurri supplies the perfect amount of spice and zest, but you can really kick up the heat by leaving in the jalapeño seeds.

▶ Preparation Time: 3 minutes | Cooking Time: 25–27 minutes | Total Time: 28–30 minutes | SERVES 6

1 x 3 to 3½lbs (1.3 to 1.5kgs) whole local heritage chicken, cut into 8 pieces
2 tablespoons duck or bacon fat
1 teaspoon sea salt
1 teaspoon freshly ground black pepper

FOR THE CHIMICHURRI

1 cup (40g/1½oz) basil leaves
1 cup (60g/2oz) cilantro leaves
1 cup (60g/2oz) parsley leaves
1 to 2 jalapeños, stemmed, seeded, and roughly chopped
1 garlic clove
2 tablespoons unfiltered apple cider vinegar
1 tablespoon Dijon mustard
1 tablespoon raw honey
½ teaspoon freshly ground black pepper
¼ teaspoon sea salt
¼ cup (60ml/2fl oz) olive oil

1. Preheat a grill or grill pan over high heat.
2. In a large bowl, add the chicken, duck or bacon fat, salt, and pepper and mix well to coat.
3. Transfer the seasoned chicken to the grill or pan and cook for 5 minutes, or until the skin begins to crust. Reduce the heat to medium-high and cook for another 10 minutes on the first side. Turn the chicken over and cook for another 10 minutes, or until chicken is cooked through.
4. In the meantime, make the chimichurri. In a food processor, combine all the ingredients and process until well mixed.
5. Plate the chicken and serve with the chimichurri sauce.

CAL 270 | CAL FROM FAT 150 | TOTAL FAT 17G | SAT FAT 3.5G | SODIUM 650MG | FIBER 1G | PRO 24G

MINI CHICKEN PATTIES WITH COCONUT SAUCE

These chicken patties are sweet, salty, spicy, and sour—all at the same time! The combination of flavors (traditional in Thai cuisine) is wonderful alongside something simple, such as sautéed greens or a fresh salad.

▶ Preparation Time: 10 minutes | Cooking Time: 12 minutes | Total Time: 22 minutes | MAKES TWENTY PATTIES

1lb (450g/16oz) organic free-range ground chicken, white and dark meat
2 organic free-range eggs
⅓ cup (35g/1¼oz) almond meal
¼ cup (20g/¾) unsweetened shredded coconut
3 scallions, white part only, chopped
2 tablespoons chili paste
2 tablespoons chopped basil
juice of 1 lime
1 tablespoon coconut oil

FOR THE SAUCE
1 cup (240ml/8fl oz) coconut milk
2 tablespoons Hot Pepper Sauce (page 197)
2 tablespoons Paleo-friendly fish sauce
2 tablespoons freshly squeezed lime juice
3 scallions, green part only, chopped

1. In a large bowl, combine the ground chicken, eggs, almond meal, coconut, scallions, chili paste, basil, and lime juice and mix well to combine. Using a tablespoon, form the mixture into twenty patties.
2. Heat the coconut oil in a large sauté pan over medium-high heat. Add the patties and cook for 4 minutes, or until browned and crispy. Flip and cook for another 4 minutes.
3. Transfer the patties to a platter and keep warm.
4. In the same sauté pan, add the coconut milk, chili sauce, fish sauce, and lime juice. Bring to a boil over medium heat, reduce the heat, and simmer for 3 minutes, stirring.
5. To serve, pour the sauce over the patties and garnish with the chopped scallions.

CAL 440 | CAL FROM FAT 300 | TOTAL FAT 34G | SAT FAT 19G | SODIUM 960MG | FIBER 2G | PRO 27G

THAI CHICKEN SKEWERS WITH SATAY SAUCE

Thai chicken skewers are great under the broiler, but they are even better on the grill! The sauce—creamy, spicy, and oh-so-good—is a delicious side to most grilled meats. Throw some fresh veggies on the grill along with the satay for color and taste.

▶ Preparation Time: 15 minutes | Cooking Time: 6 minutes | Total Time: 21 minutes | SERVES 4

¼ cup (60ml/2 fl oz) coconut aminos
2 tablespoons creamy almond butter
juice of 2 large limes
1 tablespoon curry powder
1 tablespoon minced ginger
1 garlic clove, minced
1lb (450g/16oz) organic free-range skinless chicken breasts, cut into 1" (2.5cm)-wide strips
16 x 6" (15cm) skewers, soaked in water for at least 10 minutes
½ cup (30g/1oz) cilantro leaves

FOR THE SATAY SAUCE

¾ cup (175ml/6fl oz) coconut milk
¼ cup (60ml/2fl oz) coconut aminos
¼ cup (60g/2oz) almond butter
¼ cup (60ml/2fl oz) chicken broth
1 tablespoon Green Curry Paste (page 201)
1 tablespoon fresh ginger root, minced
1 garlic clove, minced

1. Preheat a grill or the broiler on high. If broiling, line a baking sheet with aluminum foil or parchment paper.
2. In a medium bowl, whisk together the coconut milk, coconut aminos, almond butter, lime juice, curry powder, ginger, and garlic. Add the chicken and stir. Allow to marinate for 10 minutes.
3. In the meantime, make the satay sauce. In a small bowl, add all the ingredients and mix well to combine. Set aside.
4. Thread the chicken onto the skewers.
5. To grill, lay the skewers crosswise on the grill and grill for 2–3 minutes on each side. To broil, transfer the skewers to the prepared baking sheet and broil in the top third of the oven for 2–3 minutes, flip over, and broil for an additional 2–3 minutes.
6. To serve, arrange the chicken skewers on a platter and sprinkle with cilantro. Serve with the satay sauce.

CAL 390 | CAL FROM FAT 220 | TOTAL FAT 24G | SAT FAT 10G | SODIUM 180MG | FIBER 3G | PRO 29G

CHICKEN & ZUCCHINI FRITTERS WITH NECTARINE-JALAPEÑO SALSA

These fritters are light, flavorful, and simple to make—they're perfect for picnics or al fresco dining in the summer. Make sure you have a fresh nectarine that isn't too ripe, since you want the crisp texture to hold up in the salsa. And trust me, this salsa is so delicious that you'll be looking for *any* excuse to put it on top of your favorite foods.

▶ Preparation Time: 15 minutes | Cooking Time: 10 minutes | Total Time: 25 minutes | SERVES 4

1lb (450g/16oz) organic free-range ground chicken, dark and white meat
1 zucchini, coarsely grated
1 yellow or orange bell pepper, diced
½ red onion, diced
2 garlic cloves, minced
½ cup (50g/2oz) almond meal
1 organic free-range egg
1 tablespoon Dijon mustard
1 tablespoon Hot Pepper Sauce (page 197)
grated zest of ½ lime
½ teaspoon sea salt
½ teaspoon freshly ground black pepper
2 tablespoons olive oil

FOR THE SALSA

1 large nectarine, cored and diced
¼ red onion, diced
½ yellow or orange bell pepper, diced
2 tablespoons jalapeño, seeded and diced
juice of 1 lime
¼ teaspoon sea salt

1. In a large bowl, combine the ground chicken, zucchini, bell pepper, onion, garlic, almond meal, egg, Dijon, hot sauce, lime zest, salt, and pepper. Mix well to combine. With wet hands, form the mixture into eight fritters, about 3" (4.5cm) in diameter.
2. Heat the olive oil in a large sauté pan over medium-high heat. Add the fritters and cook for 5 minutes on each side. Do not touch the fritters once you add them to the pan: you want a crust to form, so just leave them to cook for the full 5 minutes before you flip them.
3. In the meantime, make the salsa. In a medium bowl, combine all the ingredients and stir to mix well. Set aside.
4. To serve, top the hot fritters with the salsa and enjoy!

CAL 380 | CAL FROM FAT 220 | TOTAL FAT 25G | SAT FAT 4.5G | SODIUM 590MG | FIBER 4G | PRO 28G

GINGER CHICKEN & VEGETABLE STIR-FRY

Stir-fries are quick to put together—I like to think of them as a "use up whatever is in your fridge" type of meal. This version has carrots, water chestnuts, bamboo shoots, bok choy, shiitake mushrooms, and celery, but feel free to use whatever is in your fridge!

▶ Preparation Time: 15 minutes | Cooking Time: 7–9 minutes | Total Time: 22–24 minutes | SERVES 4

1 lb (450g/16oz) organic free-range boneless, skinless chicken breasts, cut into bite-size pieces
1 x 1" (2.5cm) piece, fresh ginger root, peeled and minced
2 garlic cloves, minced
1 tablespoon Hot Pepper Sauce (page 197)
1 tablespoon coconut aminos
2 teaspoons, plus 1 tablespoon sesame oil
1 sweet onion, thinly sliced
1 large carrot, thinly sliced
1lb (450g/16oz) shiitake mushrooms, stemmed and sliced
6 to 8 scallions, trimmed and cut into 2" (5cm) pieces
1lb (450g/16oz) baby bok choy, cut into bite-size pieces
1 x 8oz (225ml) can water chestnuts, drained and sliced
1 x 8oz (225ml) can bamboo shoots, drained

FOR THE SAUCE

1 x 2" (5cm) piece fresh ginger root, peeled and minced
4 garlic cloves, minced
½ cup (120ml/4fl oz) chicken broth
2 tablespoons coconut aminos
1 teaspoon Hot Pepper Sauce (page 197)
1 teaspoon raw honey

1. In a medium bowl, combine the chicken, ginger, garlic, Hot Pepper Sauce, coconut aminos, and 2 teaspoons sesame oil. Set aside to marinate.
2. Heat a large wok or sauté pan over high heat. Add the marinated chicken to the hot wok and stir-fry, stirring frequently, for 2–3 minutes, or until browned and almost completely cooked through. Transfer the chicken to a clean bowl and set aside.
3. Wipe the wok clean and add the remaining 1 tablespoon sesame oil. Add the onion, carrot, mushrooms, and scallions to the wok. Stir-fry for 2–3 minutes, or until vegetables are crisp-tender.
4. Add the bok choy, water chestnuts, and bamboo shoots. Stir-fry, stirring frequently, for another 2 minutes, or until the bok choy wilts and turns bright green.
5. In a small bowl, make the sauce. Whisk together the ginger, garlic, chicken broth, coconut aminos, Hot Pepper Sauce, and honey.
6. Add the chicken and sauce to the wok, bring to a boil, and stir-fry for another minute.

CAL 550 | CAL FROM FAT 70 | TOTAL FAT 9G | SAT FAT 1.5G | SODIUM 490MG | FIBER 6G | PRO 31G

CHICKEN PAD THAI WITH ZUCCHINI NOODLES & CRUSHED CASHEWS

Zucchini noodles, chicken, bean sprouts, egg, and crushed cashews . . . it's Pad Thai gone Paleo, so how could you *not* want to make this recipe? Prepare all the ingredients in advance to save time in the kitchen: A julienne peeler, for example, is great for making zucchini noodles, although a mandoline or food processor fitted with a shredding blade will work just as well.

▶ Preparation Time: 15 minutes | Cooking Time: 15 minutes | Total Time: 30 minutes | SERVES 4

½lb (225g/8oz) organic free-range boneless, skinless chicken breasts, diced
3 tablespoons coconut aminos
1 teaspoon arrowroot
1lb (450g/16oz) zucchini
1 tablespoon vegetable or olive oil
4 garlic cloves, minced
1 jalapeño, seeded and minced
2 organic free-range eggs
1lb (450g/16oz) bean sprouts
6 to 8 scallions, sliced
1 cup (60g/2oz) cilantro leaves, to garnish
½ cup (75g/2½oz) roasted salted cashews, chopped, to garnish
1 lime, quartered, to garnish

FOR THE SAUCE

¼ cup (60ml/2fl oz) Paleo-friendly fish sauce
¼ cup (60ml/2fl oz) chicken broth
juice of 2 limes
1 to 2 tablespoons Hot Pepper Sauce (page 197), depending on desired spiciness
2 tablespoons coconut sugar

1. In a medium bowl, combine the chicken, coconut aminos, and arrowroot and mix well. Set aside.
2. To prepare the zucchini noodles, cut a thin slice lengthwise off the bottom of each zucchini to prevent them from rolling around on the cutting board. Place the flat side down on the cutting board and use the julienne peeler to shred the noodles. Set aside.
3. In a small bowl, make the sauce. Whisk together the fish sauce, chicken broth, lime juice, Hot Pepper Sauce, and coconut sugar. Set aside. Heat the oil in a large wok over high heat and add the chicken, garlic, and jalapeño. Sauté for 4–5 minutes, stirring frequently, until the chicken is cooked through.
4. Push the chicken to the sides of the wok. Crack the eggs into the center and scramble, stirring frequently, for about 1 minute, or until cooked.
5. Add the zucchini noodles and sauce to the wok. Toss until noodles are well coated and cook for 1 minute.
6. Add the bean sprouts and scallions and stir-fry for another minute.
7. To serve, plate the pad thai and garnish with cilantro leaves, chopped cashews, and lime wedges.

CAL 560 | CAL FROM FAT 140 | TOTAL FAT 16G | SAT FAT 3.5G | SODIUM 1200MG | FIBER 3G | PRO 22G

CRISPY CHICKEN WINGS

Chicken wings take much longer than 30 minutes to cook, but the secret to shaving minutes off your cooking time is eliminating the marinating time and boiling the meat. The finished product is a juicy yet crispy and flavorful chicken wing. Note: The 30-minute time here does not include the time it takes to boil the water, so start boiling the water immediately when you begin. For heightened flavor, toss the wings in some of the sauce straight out of the oven. Ready, set, go!

▶ Preparation Time: 3 minutes | Cooking Time: 25–27 minutes | Total Time: 28–30 minutes | SERVES 4

2lbs (900g/32oz) organic free-range chicken wings, wing tips removed, separated into drumsticks and wings
½ cup (120ml/4fl oz) chili paste
¼ cup (60ml/2fl oz) sesame oil
¼ cup (60ml/2fl oz) raw honey
2 tablespoons fresh ginger root, peeled and minced,
2 garlic cloves, minced
zest and juice of 1 lime
1 teaspoon sea salt

1. Preheat the oven to 450°F. Line a baking sheet with aluminum foil and place a rack on top.
2. Bring a pot of salted water to a boil over high heat. Add the chicken wings and drumsticks and boil for 5 minutes.
3. To make the sauce, whisk together the chili paste, sesame oil, honey, ginger, garlic, lime zest and juice, and salt. Divide the sauce into two bowls and set aside.
4. Drain the chicken, place on the prepared rack, and brush with the marinade from one bowl. Bake in the oven for 12 minutes.
5. Remove from the oven, turn the wings and drumsticks over, and brush with more marinade. Bake for another 12 minutes.
6. Increase the oven temperature to broil, move the baking sheet to the top rack, and broil for 1–2 minutes, or until browned and crispy.
7. Toss the chicken in the reserved marinade and serve.

CAL 420 | CAL FROM FAT 180 | TOTAL FAT 20G | SAT FAT 11G | SODIUM 1000MG | FIBER 1G | PRO 43G

BACON-WRAPPED TURKEY & SPINACH ROULADES WITH ROASTED PEPPER SAUCE

This beautifully presented dish is perfect for company, and it can be served with mashed sweet potatoes or parsnips and a salad for a well-rounded, elegant meal. You may also swap out the spinach for any of your other favorite greens.

▶ Preparation Time: 10 minutes | Cooking Time: 19–20 minutes | Total Time: 29–30 minutes | SERVES 4

1lb (450g/16oz) organic free-range turkey breast cutlets
1 teaspoon olive oil
2 cloves garlic cloves, minced
⅔lb (300g/10½oz) baby spinach
1½ teaspoons sea salt
1½ teaspoons freshly ground black pepper
8 thin slices bacon
8 toothpicks

FOR THE SAUCE

1 x 12oz (340g) jar roasted red peppers, drained
2 garlic cloves
1 cup (40g/1½oz) basil leaves
1 tablespoon balsamic vinegar
¼ cup (60ml/2fl oz) olive oil
¼ teaspoon sea salt

1. Preheat the oven to 400°F. Place the turkey cutlets, one at a time, between two pieces of plastic wrap. Using a rolling pin, gently roll out each cutlet so it measures about 9" x 4" (23cm x 10cm) and ¼" (16mm) thick. Don't worry about exact measurements. Set aside.
2. Heat the olive oil in a large ovenproof sauté pan over medium heat. Add the garlic and spinach and cook for 2–3 minutes, or until wilted. Season with ½ teaspoon each salt and pepper and set aside to cool.
3. Arrange the turkey breast cutlets on a clean dry surface. Season with 1 teaspoon each salt and pepper. Divide the cooled spinach between the four cutlets. Roll the turkey breasts around the filling and then wrap two slices of bacon around each roulade. Secure with toothpicks.

4. In the same sauté pan over medium heat, add the roulades and sear for 8 minutes, turning occasionally so all sides are seared. The bacon should be browned and crispy.
5. Transfer the pan to the preheated oven and cook for 7–8 minutes, or until cooked through.
6. In the meantime, make the sauce. In a food processor, combine the peppers, garlic, basil, balsamic vinegar, olive oil, and salt. Process for 30 seconds, or until smooth.
7. To serve, transfer the roulades to a cutting board. Remove the toothpicks and slice each roulade in half. Serve with the roasted pepper sauce.

CAL 600 | CAL FROM FAT 400 | TOTAL FAT 44G | SAT FAT 11G | SODIUM 1200MG | FIBER 6G | PRO 49G

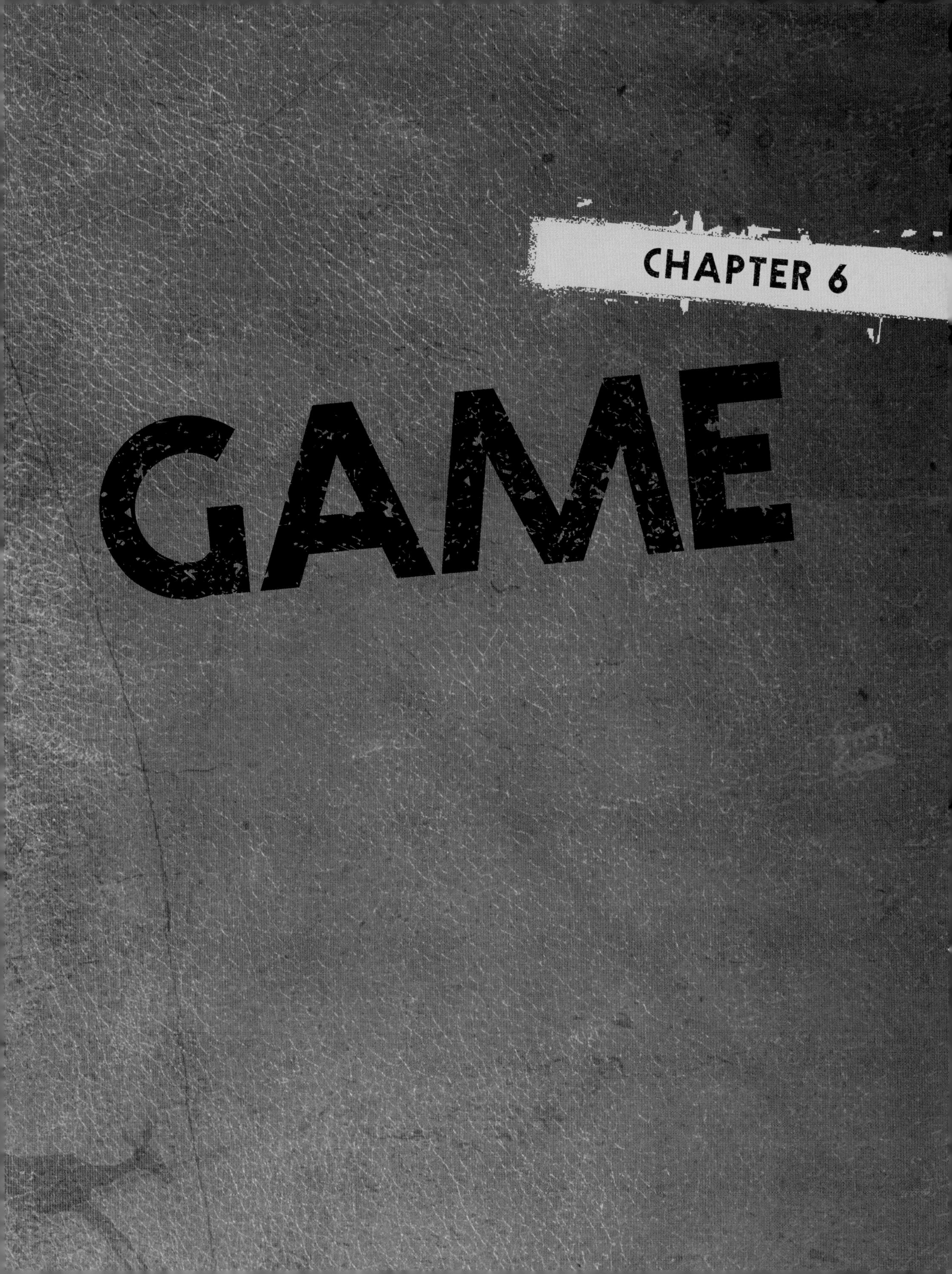

CHAPTER 6

GAME

CRISPY PAN-ROASTED DUCK BREAST WITH CHERRY-BASIL RELISH

Make sure you buy duck breasts that are around 6oz (170g) each. If they are any larger, the cooking time will increase. This is an easy recipe to prepare and utterly delicious in its simplicity.

▶ Preparation Time: 1 minute | Cooking Time: 27 minutes | Total Time: 28 minutes | SERVES 4

4 x 6oz (170g) local duck breast halves, skin scored
1 teaspoon sea salt
1 teaspoon freshly ground black pepper
½ cup (80g/2¾oz) dried cherries
¼ cup (60ml/2fl oz) dark rum or cognac
¼ cup (10g/⅓ oz) basil leaves, chopped

1. In a small bowl, soak the cherries in the dark rum or cognac. Set aside.
2. Heat a large sauté pan over medium heat until fairly hot.
3. Season both sides of the duck breasts with the salt and pepper.
4. Place the duck breasts, skin side down, in the pan. Reduce the heat to medium-low and allow the fat to render out for 20–22 minutes, removing excess fat if needed.
5. Once the fat has rendered and the skin side is golden and crispy, increase the heat to high and turn the breasts over. Cook for another 2 minutes for medium doneness.
6. Transfer the duck breasts to a cutting board, cover with foil, and allow to rest for 4–5 minutes. Reserve the pan and any juices.
7. To make the relish, drain most of the fat from the reserved pan juices and add the cherries and liquor. Simmer over medium heat, stirring occasionally, for 2–3 minutes, or until the liquid is thick and syrupy. Remove from heat and stir in the basil.
8. To serve, carve the duck into thick slices and spoon the relish over the top.

CAL 210 | CAL FROM FAT 35 | TOTAL FAT 4G | SAT FAT 1G | SODIUM 540MG | FIBER 2G | PRO 19G

QUICK BISON CHILI

Traditional chili can take up to four hours to prepare, but this recipe can be made in a fraction of the time. Quick, flavorful, and simple, it's a healthy dinner option that whips up in no time.

▶ Preparation Time: 3 minutes | Cooking Time: 25–27 minutes | Total Time: 28–30 minutes | SERVES 4

1 tablespoon olive oil
2 onions, chopped
5 garlic cloves, minced
1lb (450g/16oz) grass-fed ground bison, diced
3 tablespoons tomato paste
3 to 4 tablespoons chili powder
1 tablespoon ground cumin
1 teaspoon sea salt
½ to 1 teaspoon cayenne pepper
1 x 28oz (800g) can diced tomatoes

FOR THE TOPPING

½ onion, diced
½ cup (30g/1oz) cilantro, finely chopped
1 jalapeño, seeded and minced

1. Heat the olive oil in a large stockpot over medium-high heat. Add the onions and garlic and sauté for 3 minutes.
2. Add the bison and sauté for an additional 3 minutes, or until the bison is browned and cooked through.
3. Add the tomato paste, chili powder, cumin, salt, and cayenne. Stir for 1 minute, or until fragrant.
4. Add the diced tomatoes, bring to a boil, then reduce the heat and simmer for 15–20 minutes, stirring occasionally.
5. In the meantime, make the topping. In a small bowl, combine all the ingredients, mix, and set aside.
6. To serve, ladle the chili into bowls and serve with the topping.

CAL 350 | CAL FROM FAT 120 | TOTAL FAT 14G | SAT FAT 4.5G | SODIUM 750MG | FIBER 4G | PRO 32G

HONEY-GLAZED DUCK BREAST WITH POMEGRANATE SALSA

The addition of raw honey creates a crispy glazed duck breast—it's scrumptious! Plus, the crunch of the pomegranate seeds provides a fresh and tart contrast to the rich and fatty duck. This is one of those dishes that looks as good as it tastes.

▶ Preparation Time: 1 minute | Cooking Time: 27–29 minutes | Total Time: 28–30 minutes | SERVES 4

4 x 6oz (170g) local duck breast halves, skin scored
1 teaspoon crushed red pepper flakes
1 teaspoon sea salt
1 teaspoon freshly ground black pepper
1 tablespoon raw honey
1 pomegranate, seeds only
½ cup (30g/1oz) mixed micro herbs (such as chives, chervil, parsley, basil, or dill)

1. Heat a large sauté pan over medium heat until fairly hot.
2. Season both sides of the duck breasts with the red pepper flakes, salt, and black pepper.
3. Place the duck breasts, skin side down, in the pan. Reduce the heat to medium-low and allow the fat to render out for 18–20 minutes, removing excess fat if needed and reserving 1 teaspoon fat for use in the salsa.
4. Once the fat has rendered and the skin side is golden and crispy, drizzle with the honey, then increase heat to medium-high and cook for 1 minute to create the caramelized crust. Flip the duck breasts over and cook for another minute for medium-rare doneness.
5. Transfer the duck to a cutting board, cover with foil, and allow to rest for 4–5 minutes. Reserve the pan and any juices.
6. To make the salsa, combine the pomegranate seeds, herbs, and the reserved duck fat in a small bowl and mix well.
7. To serve, carve the duck into thick slices and spoon the pomegranate salsa over the top.

CAL 160 | CAL FROM FAT 45 | TOTAL FAT 5G | SAT FAT 1.5G | SODIUM 530MG | FIBER 1G | PRO 19G

QUICK VEAL TAGINE

Tagines traditionally cook for long time periods, similar to a braise, but this dish is super quick and explodes with flavor. If you don't like veal, try it with a similar tender cut of meat such as beef or venison fillet.

▶ Preparation Time: 5 minutes | Cooking Time: 25 minutes | Total Time: 30 minutes | SERVES 4

1lb (450g/16oz) veal tenderloin, cut into 1" (2.5cm) pieces
grated zest and juice of 1 small lemon
1 teaspoon ground cinnamon
1 teaspoon ground cumin
½ teaspoon sea salt
½ teaspoon cayenne pepper
2 tablespoons olive oil
1 sweet onion, diced
2 carrots, sliced diagonally
2 garlic cloves, minced
1½ cups (350ml/12fl oz) chicken broth
½ cup (90g/3oz) pitted prunes
½ cup (75g/2½oz) whole blanched almonds
1 teaspoon saffron threads
¼ cup (15g/½oz) cilantro leaves

1. In a medium bowl, combine the veal, lemon zest, lemon juice, cinnamon, cumin, salt, and cayenne and mix well. Allow to marinate for 5 minutes.
2. In a tagine pan or large saucepan, heat the olive oil over medium-high heat. Add the onions, carrots, and garlic and sauté for 3 minutes, stirring occasionally.
3. Add the marinated meat, along with the juices, and cook for another 3 minutes.
4. Add the chicken broth, prunes, ¼ cup (38g) almonds, and saffron to the pan. Bring to a boil, cover, and reduce the heat to low. Simmer for 15 minutes.
5. Remove the lid and simmer for another 3 minutes.
6. While the tagine is simmering, combine the remaining ¼ cup (38g) almonds and cilantro in a small food processor and pulse to finely chop.
7. To serve, ladle the tagine into bowls and top with the cilantro-almond mixture.

CAL 390 | CAL FROM FAT 180 | TOTAL FAT 20G | SAT FAT 2.5G | SODIUM 470MG | FIBER 5G | PRO 29G

BISON, FIG & MUSHROOM KEBABS WITH CILANTRO-JALAPEÑO PESTO

Cook these delicious kebabs 3 minutes per side for medium rare or 4 minutes for medium. Sweet fig, earthy mushrooms, and tasty bison team up wonderfully, but the addition of fresh and spicy cilantro-jalapeño pesto makes this a must-try dish!

▶ Preparation Time: 5 minutes | Cooking Time: 6–8 minutes | Total Time: 11–13 minutes | SERVES 4

1lb (450g/16oz) bison rib-eye steaks, trimmed and cut into 1" (2.5cm) pieces
1 tablespoon bacon or duck fat
1 teaspoon ground cumin
1 teaspoon freshly ground black pepper
16 x 6" (15cm) bamboo skewers, soaked in water for 5 minutes
16 fresh figs, tops removed
8 crimini mushrooms, halved

FOR THE PESTO
1 cup (60g/2oz) cilantro leaves
1 jalapeño, seeded and chopped
1 garlic clove
2 tablespoons unfiltered apple cider vinegar
1 teaspoon raw honey
¼ teaspoon sea salt
¼ cup (60ml/2fl oz) olive oil

1. Preheat a skillet or grill pan over high heat.
2. In a medium bowl, combine the bison, bacon or duck fat, cumin, salt, and peppers and mix well.
3. To make the skewers, skewer a fig, cut side up, followed by a piece of bison, a mushroom half, and another piece of bison. Repeat with the remaining skewers.
4. Add the skewers to the skillet or grill pan and cook 3–4 minutes per side, depending on desired doneness.
5. In the meantime, make the pesto. In a food processor, combine the cilantro, jalapeño, garlic, vinegar, honey, and salt and process until smooth. Slowly drizzle in the olive oil and process until incorporated.
6. To serve, plate the skewers and drizzle the pesto over the top.

CAL 500 | CAL FROM FAT 230 | TOTAL FAT 25G | SAT FAT 6G | SODIUM 710MG | FIBER 6G | PRO 25G

BUFFALO BURGER WITH CARAMELIZED ONIONS, MUSHROOMS & LETTUCE

Burgers are such a simple and wonderful way to make your family happy for a weeknight dinner. This one is perfection with its charred tender buffalo, sweet onions, and sliced mushrooms, all encased in a crisp and fresh butter lettuce "bun." Enjoy!

▶ Preparation Time: 5 minutes | Cooking Time: 20 minutes | Total Time: 25 minutes | SERVES 4

2 tablespoons olive oil, divided
3 cups (225g/8oz) crimini mushrooms, sliced
1 sweet yellow onion, thinly sliced
1lb (450g/16oz) ground buffalo
2 tablespoons Dijon mustard
2 garlic cloves, minced
1 teaspoon sea salt
1 teaspoon freshly ground black pepper
4 Boston lettuce leaves
4 tablespoons spicy brown mustard

1. Heat 1 tablespoon olive oil in a large sauté pan over medium-high heat.
2. Add the mushrooms and onion and sauté for 10–12 minutes, stirring occasionally, or until browned and caramelized. Transfer to a bowl and keep warm.
3. In a large bowl, combine the buffalo, Dijon, garlic, salt, and pepper and mix well. Form into four patties.
4. Heat the remaining tablespoon of olive oil in the same pan over medium-high heat.
5. Add the patties and cook for 3–5 minutes on each side, depending on desired doneness.
6. To serve, place a lettuce leaf on each plate, drizzle the mustard onto each leaf, and top with a burger. Finish with the onion-mushroom topping.

CAL 310 | CAL FROM FAT 140 | TOTAL FAT 16G | SAT FAT 4.5G | SODIUM 1120MG | FIBER 3G | PRO 27G

SPICE-CRUSTED GRILLED ELK RIB CHOP

Elk is a lean, all-natural red meat that is lower in fat and cholesterol than traditional red meat. It also holds up really well under strong flavors, like those in this spicy crust. If you like things spicier, feel free to up the chili powder and cayenne pepper in the crust mixture.

▶ Preparation Time: 15 minutes | Cooking Time: 7–11 minutes | Total Time: 22–26 minutes | SERVES 4

1 tablespoon cumin seeds
1 tablespoon fennel seeds
1 tablespoon coriander seeds
3 tablespoons paprika
2 tablespoons chili powder
1 tablespoon dried oregano
2 teaspoons sea salt
2 teaspoons freshly ground black pepper
1 teaspoon dried thyme
1 teaspoon cayenne pepper
4 x 6oz (170g) elk rib chops
2 tablespoons olive oil

1. In a small sauté pan over low heat, add the cumin seeds, fennel seeds, and coriander seeds. Toast for 3 minutes, or until fragrant.
2. Transfer to a spice grinder and add the paprika, chili powder, oregano, salt, pepper, thyme, and cayenne. Grind until well combined and fine.
3. Rub the spice mixture over the rib chops and marinate for 10 minutes.
4. In the meantime, heat the olive oil in a large skillet over medium-high heat.
5. Add the marinated chops to the skillet and cook for 2–4 minutes. Flip and cook for another 2–4 minutes, depending on your preferred doneness. Enjoy!

CAL 260 | CAL FROM FAT 90 | TOTAL FAT 10G | SAT FAT 2G | SODIUM 1060MG | FIBER 0G | PRO 39G

VENISON FLANK STEAK ROULADE STUFFED WITH HERB PESTO

Because venison flank steak is small, I often overlap the pieces to create a thin, wide piece of meat that's ideal for a beautiful roulade. Venison is best served rare, but if you like your meat more well done, just increase the cooking time on each side.

▶ Preparation Time: 5 minutes | Cooking Time: 6–9 minutes, plus 5 minutes resting time
Total Time: 16–19 minutes | SERVES 4

1½lbs (675g/24oz) venison flank steak
1 teaspoon sea salt
1 teaspoon freshly ground black pepper
⅓ cup (15g/½oz) tarragon leaves
⅓ cup (20g/¾oz) parsley leaves
2 garlic cloves
½ jalapeño, seeded
kitchen twine
2 tablespoons olive oil

1. Lay out the steak on a clean dry surface, overlapping the pieces to create one large flat piece of venison. The seams should be parallel to you.
2. Season the steak with ½ teaspoon each salt and pepper.
3. In a small food processor, combine the tarragon, parsley, garlic, jalapeño, and remaining ½ teaspoon each salt and pepper. Pulse until finely chopped and well combined.
4. Spread the herb mixture on the top three-quarters of the steak. Starting from the top, roll the steak toward you (where there is no filling) to create a roulade.
5. Using the twine, make three or four knots along the steak roulade to hold it together.
6. Heat the olive oil in a large sauté pan over medium-high heat. Add the roulade and cook for 2–3 minutes per side, turning a total of three times to sear all sides. You want a nice deep-brown crust.
7. Transfer to a cutting board, cover loosely with aluminum foil, and allow to rest for 5 minutes.
8. To serve, remove the twine and slice the roulade into eight pieces. Enjoy!

CAL 280 | CAL FROM FAT 100 | TOTAL FAT 11G | SAT FAT 2.5G | SODIUM 580MG | FIBER 0G | PRO 40G

EMU, KALE & SWEET POTATO SHEPHERD'S PIE

This is a wonderfully delicious take on the classic shepherd's pie, and it may just become one of your new favorites. To play with the dish even further, you could add parsnips to the mash or even try Swiss chard or spinach instead of kale. Also consider using up leftover mashed potatoes or sautéed greens, which will make this simple recipe even quicker to prepare. If you can't find emu, substitute with ground bison, venison, or even beef.

▶ Preparation Time: 5 minutes | Cooking Time: 25 minutes | Total Time: 30 minutes | SERVES 6

olive oil spray
1½lbs (675g/24oz) sweet potatoes, peeled and diced
4 garlic cloves, 2 smashed and 2 minced
2 cups (475ml/16fl oz) chicken broth
1½ teaspoons sea salt, divided
1½teaspoons freshly ground black pepper, divided
1½ tablespoons olive oil, plus extra for greasing, divided
½ sweet onion, diced
1lb (450g/16oz) ground emu chopped
1 tablespoon rosemary, finely chopped
1 tablespoon thyme, finely chopped
1 cup (240ml/8fl oz) Homemade Marinara (page 185)
2lbs (900g/32oz) kale, torn into bite-size pieces

1. Preheat the oven to broil. Spray an 8" (20cm)-square baking pan with olive oil spray. In a medium saucepan over high heat, combine the sweet potatoes, smashed garlic, chicken broth, and ½ teaspoon each salt, and pepper. Bring to a boil, then reduce heat to medium-high and cook for 15 minutes, or until potatoes are soft.
2. In the meantime, prepare the meat filling. Heat 1 tablespoon olive oil in a large sauté pan over medium heat. Add the onion and sauté, stirring frequently, for 3 minutes, or until translucent and lightly browning. Add the remaining minced garlic to the onion and stir for 30 seconds, or until fragrant. Add the ground emu, rosemary, and thyme. Cook, stirring frequently, for 3–4 minutes, or until the meat is browned and cooked through. Stir in the Homemade Marinara and cook for 2 minutes, or until warmed through. Season with the remaining salt and pepper.
3. While the potatoes and emu are cooking, make the wilted greens. Heat the remaining ½ tablespoon olive oil in a large sauté pan over medium heat. Add the kale, cover, and sauté, stirring occasionally, for 2–3 minutes, or until wilted. Season with ½ teaspoon each salt and pepper.
4. To make the mashed sweet potatoes, use a handheld mixer or an immersion blender to whip the sweet potatoes and chicken broth until mashed and creamy.
5. To assemble the shepherd's pie, spoon the emu mixture into the bottom of the prepared pan. Top with the wilted greens and spread the mashed sweet potatoes on top. Broil for 2–4 minutes, or until bubbly and lightly browned on top. Serve immediately.

CAL 310 | CAL FROM FAT 70 | TOTAL FAT 8G | SAT FAT 1.5G | SODIUM 1180MG | FIBER 7G | PRO 25G

EGGPLANT & GROUND VENISON BAKE

The layered meat sauce, roasted eggplant, and ground artichoke-nut "cheese" resemble the delectable layers of a lasagna—and they're just as tasty! You may swap out the venison for any other ground meat of your choice: Bison, beef, emu, or ostrich are all great choices.

▶ Preparation Time: 5 minutes | Cooking Time: 25 minutes | Total Time: 30 minutes | SERVES 8

1 tablespoon olive oil, plus extra for greasing
1lb (450g/16oz) eggplant, cut into ⅛" (3mm) slices
2 teaspoons sea salt
½ sweet onion, diced
4 garlic cloves, minced
1lb (450g/16oz) organic grass-fed ground venison
1 cup (240ml/8fl oz) dry red wine
4 cups (950ml/32fl oz) Homemade Marinara (page 185)
1 teaspoon freshly ground black pepper
⅔ cup (100g/3½oz) raw cashews
1 cup (135g/4¾oz) pine nuts, toasted
1½ x 9oz (400g) package frozen artichoke hearts, thawed
1 cup (40g/1½oz) basil leaves

1. Preheat the oven to broil. Line a baking sheet with aluminum foil. Grease four mini loaf pans with olive oil and place on the baking sheet.
2. Place a rack on top of another baking sheet. Arrange the eggplant slices in a single layer on the rack and season with ½ teaspoon salt. Transfer the baking sheet to the broiler and cook for 5 minutes. Remove from the oven and set aside.
3. Heat remaining 1 tablespoon olive oil in a large sauté pan over medium-high heat. Add the onion and sauté for 3 minutes, stirring occasionally. Add the garlic and ground venison and cook, stirring occasionally, for 4 minutes, or until browned and cooked through.
4. Add the wine to the pan and simmer for 2 minutes, stirring occasionally. Add the Homemade Marinara, 1 teaspoon salt, and ½ teaspoon pepper and cook for another minute, or until heated through. Remove from heat.
5. To make the nut "cheese," combine the cashews and pine nuts in a food processor and process for 30 seconds, or until finely chopped. Add the artichoke hearts, basil, and remaining ½ teaspoon each salt and pepper and process again for 30 seconds, or until well combined.
6. To make the lasagna, spoon some of the meat sauce into the bottom of a greased loaf pan. Layer with two eggplant slices, a quarter of the nut mixture, more meat sauce, two more eggplant slices, and lastly a little more meat sauce. Repeat with the remaining loaf pans. Cover the four bakes with foil and bake for 10 minutes at 475 °F. Uncover and bake another 5 minutes. Serve hot!

CAL 450 | CAL FROM FAT 130 | TOTAL FAT 15G | SAT FAT 2.5G | SODIUM 870MG | FIBER 12G | PRO 23G

OSTRICH SCALOPPINI WITH PROSCIUTTO & SAGE

Traditionally, this dish is made with thinly pounded veal; the reinterpretation here features ostrich flavored with sage and prosciutto for a tasty and healthy meal.

▶ Preparation Time: 8 minutes | Cooking Time: 9–13 minutes Total Time: 17–21 minutes | SERVES 4

1lb (450g/16oz) ostrich fillets
1 teaspoon sea salt
1 teaspoon freshly ground black pepper
2 garlic cloves, thinly sliced
8 slices prosciutto
8 sage leaves
8 toothpicks
1 tablespoon olive oil
1 cup (240ml/8fl oz) dry red wine

1. Slice the ostrich fillets into eight thin slices, about ⅛" (3mm) thick.
2. Season the ostrich with salt, pepper, and garlic. Lay a slice of prosciutto and 1 sage leaf on the top quarter of each ostrich slice.
3. Starting from the top, roll the slice toward you to create a tightly rolled roulade. Fasten with a toothpick and repeat with the remaining fillets.
4. Heat the olive oil in a large sauté pan over medium-high heat. Add the ostrich roulades and cook for 2–3 minutes per side, turning a total of three times to cook all sides. Transfer the roulades to a platter, cover with aluminum foil, and allow to rest for 3 minutes.
5. To make the sauce, add the wine to the same sauté pan and cook for 1 minute, scraping up the browned bits on the bottom. Once the sauce has thickened slightly and reduced by half, pour over the ostrich roulades.
6. Remove the toothpicks and serve!

CAL 280 | CAL FROM FAT 90 | TOTAL FAT 10G | SAT FAT 3G | SODIUM 1000MG | FIBER 0G | PRO 33G

THAI ANTELOPE WITH BASIL & CHILIES

Antelope meat is a great source of protein and an incredible source of heme iron. The secret to this dish is to have all the ingredients prepped and ready to go—then the meal will come together in a flash! The combination of flavors here is wonderful. Leave the chili seeds in the dish if you prefer it extra spicy. And if you can't find antelope, venison is a great substitute.

▶ Preparation Time: 10 minutes | Cooking Time: 10 minutes | Total Time: 20 minutes | SERVES 4

2 tablespoons Paleo-friendly fish sauce
2 tablespoons coconut aminos
2 tablespoons freshly squeezed lime juice
1 tablespoon raw honey
1 tablespoon filtered water
2 tablespoons sesame oil, divided
4 garlic cloves, minced
3 to 5 bird's eye chilies, seeds removed and finely chopped
1lb (450g/16oz) antelope backstrap, thinly sliced
1 onion, sliced
3 cups (90g/3oz) Thai basil leaves

1. In a small bowl, combine the fish sauce, coconut aminos, lime juice, honey, and water. Mix well and set aside.
2. Heat 1 tablespoon sesame oil in a wok over high heat. Add the garlic and chilies and stir-fry for 10 seconds, or until fragrant. Add the sliced antelope and sauté, stirring frequently, for 1–2 minutes, or until no longer pink. Transfer the antelope to a plate, cover, and set aside.
3. Add the remaining tablespoon of sesame oil to the wok. Once hot, add the onions and fish sauce mixture. Stir-fry for 2 minutes, or until the onions are lightly browned and softened. Add the antelope and stir to heat through. Stir in the basil leaves and serve immediately.

CAL 490 | CAL FROM FAT 80 | TOTAL FAT 9G | SAT FAT 2G | SODIUM 790MG | FIBER 1G | PRO 27G

CHAPTER 7

VEGETABLES & SIDES

ROASTED CAULIFLOWER & POMEGRANATE WITH TAHINI SAUCE

This dish could not be any more simple or delicious! Creamy tahini sauce, caramelized and crispy cauliflower, and refreshing pomegranate seeds work perfectly together in this unbelievable combination. For a complete meal, try this side dish with one of the game recipes such as Bison, Fig & Mushroom Kebabs with Cilantro Jalapeño Pesto (page 126) or Ostrich Scallopini with Prosciutto & Sage (page 133).

▶ Preparation Time: 5 minutes | Cooking Time: 15 minutes | Total Time: 20 minutes | SERVES 4

1 cauliflower head, florets only
1 tablespoon olive oil
1 teaspoon sea salt
1 teaspoon freshly ground black pepper
1 small pomegranate, seeds only
¼ cup (15g/½oz) cilantro leaves

FOR THE SAUCE

¼ cup (60ml/2fl oz) tahini
juice of 2 lemons
½ teaspoon sea salt
¼ teaspoon cayenne pepper

1. Preheat the oven to 425°F. Line a baking sheet with parchment paper.
2. In a large bowl, combine the cauliflower florets, olive oil, salt, and pepper and toss to coat. Spread the florets on the prepared baking sheet and bake in the oven for 15 minutes, or until browned and tender.
3. In the meantime, make the sauce. In a small bowl, whisk together the tahini, lemon juice, salt, and cayenne until it comes together. Set aside.
4. Transfer the roasted cauliflower to a platter, drizzle with the sauce, and sprinkle with pomegranate seeds and cilantro leaves. Serve immediately or at room temperature.

CAL 170 | CAL FROM FAT 110 | TOTAL FAT 12G | SAT FAT 1.5G | SODIUM 760MG | FIBER 4G | PRO 5G

BABAGANOUSH

Traditional babaganoush takes a long time to roast in the oven. This one cuts down on the cook time since you peel and chop the eggplant prior to roasting. Serve this as a dip with crudités or alongside a piece of grilled chicken, steak, or pork. So versatile!

▶ Preparation Time: 3 minutes | Cook Time: 25 minutes | Total Time: 30 minutes
MAKES ABOUT 2 CUPS (475ml/16fl oz)

1 large eggplant, peeled and chopped
2 garlic cloves, smashed
3 tablespoons olive oil, divided
1 teaspoon sea salt
¼ cup (60ml/2fl oz) tahini
¼ cup (15g/½oz) cilantro leaves
1 tablespoon ground cumin
juice of 1 lemon

1. Preheat the oven to 425°F. Line a large baking sheet with aluminum foil.
2. In a large bowl, combine the eggplant, garlic, 1 tablespoon olive oil, and salt and toss to coat. Arrange on the prepared baking sheet and roast in the oven for 25 minutes, or until browned and tender.
3. In a food processor, add the roasted eggplant, tahini, cilantro, cumin, lemon juice, and remaining 2 tablespoons olive oil. Pulse 10–15 times, or until smooth but not a paste.
4. Serve warm or at room temperature.

CAL 140 | CAL FROM FAT 110 | TOTAL FAT 12G | SAT FAT 1.5G | SODIUM 330MG | FIBER 3G | PRO 3G

ZUCCHINI RIBBONS WITH GARLIC & MINT

This is an easy and elegant way to use up zucchini from the farmers' market during the late summer. Feel free to experiment with different herbs in this dish—basil and oregano also work well with zucchini. This side pairs well with a number of dishes, including Crispy Pan Roasted Duck Breast with Cherry-Basil Relish (page 121) and Spice-Crusted Grilled Elk Rib Chop (page 128).

▶ Preparation Time: 7–10 minutes | Cook Time: 5 minutes | Total Time: 12–15 minutes | SERVES 4

1 tablespoon olive oil
2 garlic cloves, minced
2 large zucchinis, trimmed and thinly sliced with a mandoline
¼ cup (10g/⅓oz) chopped mint leaves
1 teaspoon sea salt
1 teaspoon freshly ground black pepper

1. Heat the olive oil in a large sauté pan over medium heat.
2. Add the garlic and stir until fragrant, about 30 seconds.
3. Add the zucchini ribbons and sauté for 5 minutes. Season with mint, salt, and pepper, and serve.

CAL 35 | CAL FROM FAT 30 | TOTAL FAT 3.5G | SAT FAT 0G | SODIUM 480MG | FIBER 0G | PRO 0G

ROASTED SPAGHETTI SQUASH

This spaghetti replacement is great under meatballs and the Homemade Marinara (page 185) or alone as a side dish. Make sure you choose a small squash—if it's too big, it will take a lot longer to roast.

▶ Preparation Time: 1 minute | Cooking Time: 25–27 minutes | Total Time: 26–28 minutes | SERVES 4

1 small spaghetti squash
1 tablespoon duck fat
1 tablespoon thyme leaves, chopped
1 teaspoon sea salt
½ teaspoon freshly ground black pepper

1. Preheat the oven to 450°F. Line a small baking sheet with aluminum foil.
2. Pierce the squash all over with a sharp knife and place on the prepared baking sheet. Roast in the oven for 13 minutes, then rotate the squash halfway and roast for another 12–14 minutes, or until tender.
3. Remove from the oven and cut the squash in half lengthwise. Remove the seeds and discard.
4. Using a fork, scoop the flesh into a large bowl. Stir in the duck fat, thyme, salt, and pepper and serve.

CAL 60 | CAL FROM FAT 30 | TOTAL FAT 3.5G | SAT FAT 1G | SODIUM 500MG | FIBER 2G | PRO 1G

BABY BOK CHOY WITH GINGER & SESAME

Baby bok choy is tender and delicious. If you can't find any baby varieties in your local grocery, however, you may substitute one or two large ones of the same weight, chopping it into bite-sized pieces to help speed up the cooking process. For a complete meal, serve this side dish with a game recipe such as Thai Antelope with Basil & Chilies (page 134) or a fish dish such as Thai Fish Cakes with Cucumber Relish (page 59).

▶ Preparation Time: 3 minutes | Cooking Time: 4 minutes | Total Time: 7 minutes | SERVES 4

1 tablespoon sesame oil
1 tablespoon fresh ginger root, minced
2lbs (900g/32oz) baby bok choy, ends trimmed
1 tablespoon wheat-free tamari
1 teaspoon sesame seeds

1. Heat the sesame oil in a large sauté pan or wok over medium-high heat.
2. Add the ginger and stir for 30 seconds or or until fragrant.
3. Add the bok choy and cook, stirring occasionally, for about 3 minutes, or until wilted and crisp-tender.
4. Season with tamari and sesame seeds and serve.

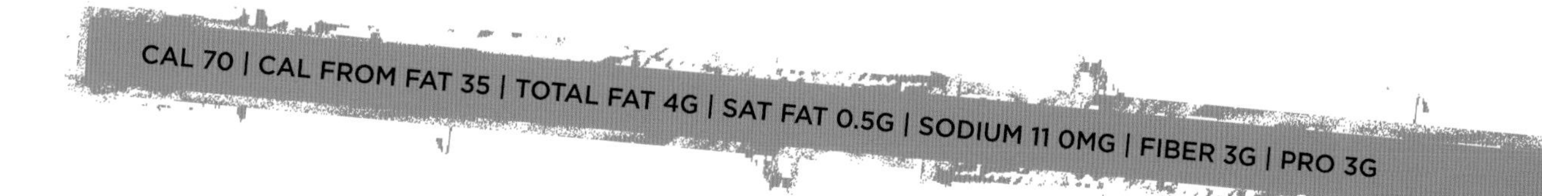

ROASTED ASPARAGUS WITH PROSCIUTTO

I try to eat asparagus as much as possible during its short season. I prefer pencil-thin spring asparagus, but if you like your asparagus thicker, then by all means go for it! Just increase the cooking time by 2–3 minutes, depending on thickness. This dish is perfect with Rosemary Shrimp Skewers (page 61), Blackened Halibut with Mango Salsa (page 70), or Spicy Mini Meatloaves (page 77). It's so versatile that the options are endless.

▶ Preparation Time: 5 minutes | Cooking Time: 12–15 minutes | Total Time: 17–20 minutes
SERVES 4–6

4oz (120g) prosciutto, thinly sliced
2lbs (900g/32oz) thin asparagus, trimmed
1 teaspoon olive oil
1 teaspoon balsamic vinegar
½ teaspoon sea salt
1 teaspoon freshly ground black pepper

1. Preheat the oven to 425°F. Line two large baking sheets with parchment paper or aluminum foil.
2. Arrange the prosciutto in a single layer on a prepared baking sheet and bake in the oven for 12–15 minutes, or until browned and crispy.
3. In a large bowl, add the asparagus, olive oil, balsamic vinegar, salt, and pepper and toss to combine. Arrange in a single layer on the other baking sheet and roast in the oven for 10–12 minutes, or until the asparagus are lightly caramelized and tender.
4. To serve, arrange the asparagus on a platter and crumble the crispy prosciutto on top.

CAL 120 | CAL FROM FAT 40 | TOTAL FAT 4.5G | SAT FAT 1.5G | SODIUM 1000MG | FIBER 5G | PRO 13G

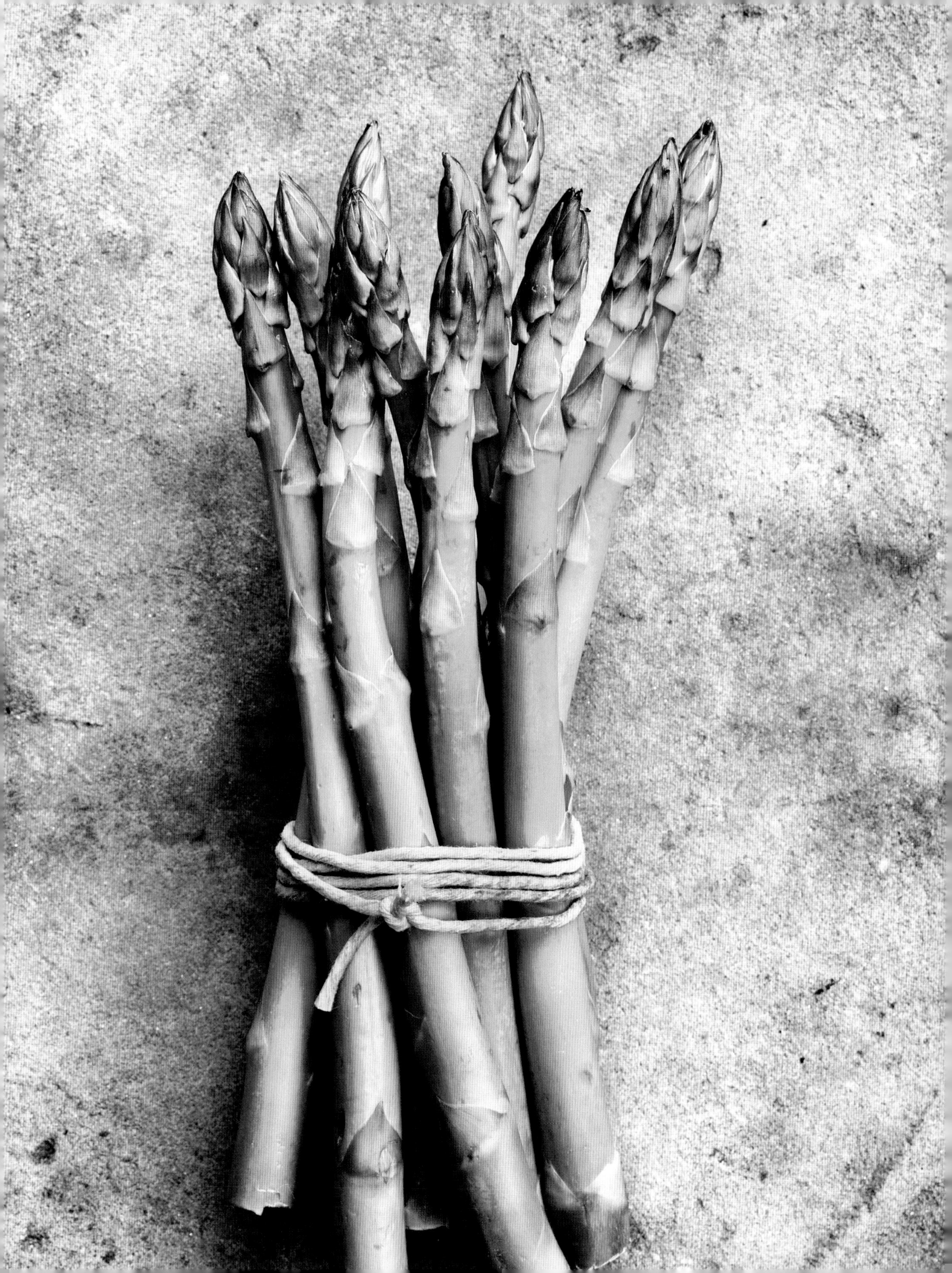

SPINACH & ARTICHOKE HEART "SOUFFLÉ"

Although this recipe is very distinct from a traditional soufflé, there is something about its flavor, lightness, and all-around superb tastiness of this dish that is sure to make it your go-to favorite! The ground raw cashews take the place of the mayonnaise and Parmesan in the traditional version of this dish, but you won't miss those two things one little bit. I confess that I am slightly obsessed with this recipe, and I'm sure you'll love it too!

▶ Preparation Time: 2 minutes | Cooking Time: 25 minutes | Total Time: 27 minutes | SERVES 8

2 tablespoons olive oil, plus extra for greasing
4 garlic cloves, minced
1 x 9oz (255g) package frozen artichoke hearts, thawed
1 bunch baby spinach
1 cup (150g/5oz) cashews
¼ cup (10g/⅓oz) basil leaves
1 teaspoon sea salt
1 teaspoon freshly ground black pepper
¼ to ½ teaspoon cayenne pepper

1. Preheat the oven to 425°F. Grease an 8" (20cm) square baking dish.
2. Heat the oil in a large sauté pan over medium heat. Add garlic and stir for 10 seconds, or until fragrant.
3. Add the artichoke hearts and spinach and sauté, stirring occasionally, for 3–4 minutes, or until the spinach is wilted.
4. In a food processor, add the cashews and process until finely ground. Add the spinach mixture, basil, salt, pepper, and cayenne and process for another minute, or until finely chopped.
5. Transfer the mixture to the prepared baking dish and bake in the oven for 20 minutes, or until the sides are golden and crispy. Serve immediately.

CAL 160 | CAL FROM FAT 110 | TOTAL FAT 12G | SAT FAT 2G | SODIUM 330MG | FIBER 4G | PRO 5G

CARROT FRIES WITH AVOCADO AIOLI

Carrot fries are always a big hit with my clients. Make sure you eat them immediately out of the oven (though I can't imagine that'll be a problem). The carrot fries can be served with one of the burgers in the game or beef chapters for a complete and satisfying meal. A traditional aioli contains eggs, but this one is simply avocado, which has the same creamy texture as a traditional aioli.

▶ Preparation Time: 5 minutes | Cooking Time: 23–25 minutes | Total Time: 28–30 minutes | SERVES 4

4 large carrots, cut into 3" x ¼" (7.5cm x 0.5cm) matchsticks
1 tablespoon duck fat
1 teaspoon sea salt
1 teaspoon freshly ground black pepper

FOR THE AIOLI
1 avocado, halved, pitted, and flesh scooped out
juice of 2 lemons
¼ cup (60ml/2fl oz) filtered water
½ teaspoon sea salt

1. Preheat the oven to 425°F. Line two baking sheets with parchment paper.
2. In a large bowl, combine the carrots, duck fat, salt, and pepper and toss to coat.
3. Arrange the carrots in a single layer on the prepared baking sheets. Bake in the oven for 15 minutes, stir the carrots, and bake for another 8–10 minutes.
4. In the meantime, make the aioli. In a food processor, combine the avocado flesh, lemon juice, water, and salt and process until smooth.
5. Serve the carrot fries immediately with the avocado aioli.

CAL 140 | CAL FROM FAT 90 | TOTAL FAT 11G | SAT FAT 2G | SODIUM 780MG | FIBER 5G | PRO 2G

ROASTED BRUSSELS SPROUTS WITH PANCETTA & GARLIC

Caramelized Brussels sprouts and pancetta make a winning combination, and this dish is truly divine. Serve with Bacon-Wrapped Turkey & Spinach Roulades with Roasted Pepper Sauce (page 116) or Bacon-Mustard-Wrapped Pork Tenderloin with Sautéed Apples (page 94).

▶ Preparation Time: 5 minutes | Cooking Time: 20–25 minutes | Total Time: 25–30 minutes | SERVES 6

1¾lbs (800g/28oz) Brussels sprouts, halved
2 teaspoons olive oil
4oz (120g) pancetta, diced
½ teaspoon sea salt
1 teaspoon freshly ground black pepper

1. Preheat the oven to 450°F. Line a baking sheet with parchment paper or aluminum foil.
2. In a large bowl, combine the Brussels sprouts, olive oil, pancetta, salt, and pepper and toss to combine.
3. Arrange the Brussels sprouts on the prepared baking sheet and roast in the oven for 20–25 minutes, or until the pancetta is crispy and the Brussels sprouts are caramelized and tender. Enjoy!

CAL 130 | CAL FROM FAT 30 | TOTAL FAT 3.5G | SAT FAT 1G | SODIUM 420MG | FIBER 3G | PRO 15G

ROASTED WILD MUSHROOMS WITH THYME

Shiitake, crimini, royal trumpet, oyster, maiitake . . . I love mushrooms, and roasting them brings out their natural sweetness through caramelization. These roasted wild mushrooms are best served on their own or with a grilled steak. When preparing your mushrooms, wipe them clean with a damp paper towel after washing. Their sponges and caps should ideally be dry for quicker and more efficient roasting.

▶ Preparation Time: 5 minutes | Cooking Time: 25 minutes | Total Time: 30 minutes | SERVES 4

2lbs (900g/32oz) mixed wild mushrooms, stemmed and quartered
2 tablespoons duck fat or olive oil
1 teaspoon sea salt
1 teaspoon freshly ground black pepper
1 teaspoon dried thyme

1. Preheat the oven to 425°F. Line two baking sheets with parchment paper or aluminum foil.
2. In a large bowl, combine the mushrooms, duck fat or oil, salt, pepper, and thyme and mix well. Arrange the mushrooms on the prepared baking sheets and spread out evenly.
3. Roast for 25 minutes and serve warm.

CAL 110 | CAL FROM FAT 70 | TOTAL FAT 7G | SAT FAT 1G | SODIUM 490MG | FIBER 1G | PRO 6G

SPICY BAKED SWEET POTATO FRIES

These crispy and delicious fries are both spicy and sweet! Serve with your favorite burger—my clients love these paired with the Buffalo Burger with Caramelized Onions, Mushrooms & Lettuce (page 127). Avoid rinsing the potatoes before peeling them: The oil won't stick to the potatoes and then you won't be able to get a crispy fry.

▶ Preparation Time: 8 minutes | Cooking Time: 22 minutes | Total Time: 30 minutes | SERVES 4

3 sweet potatoes, peeled and cut into ½" x 2" (1.3cm x 5cm) matchsticks
2 tablespoons olive oil or fat of your choice
½ to 1 tablespoon cayenne pepper
1½ teaspoons sea salt
1 teaspoon smoked paprika
1 teaspoon freshly ground black pepper
Homemade Ketchup (page 200), to serve

1. Preheat the oven to 450°F. Line two baking sheets with parchment paper.
2. In a large bowl, combine the potatoes, oil, cayenne, salt, paprika, and pepper and toss well to coat. Transfer to the prepared baking sheets.
3. Bake for 12 minutes, stir, and rotate the baking sheets, then bake for another 10 minutes.
4. Serve hot with Homemade Ketchup or your favorite dipping sauce.

CAL 200 | CAL FROM FAT 70 | TOTAL FAT 7G | SAT FAT 1G | SODIUM 780MG | FIBER 5G | PRO 3G

ROASTED GARLIC MASHED CAULIFLOWER

This is a fun twist on the original. You can't compare it to mashed potatoes, but you can feel better knowing it's a much healthier and lighter alternative. Plus, it's awesome and super comforting and pairs well with the Spicy Mini Meatloaves (page 77) and the Venison Flank Steak Roulade Stuffed with Herb Pesto (page 129).

▶ Preparation Time: 10 minutes | Cooking Time: 20 minutes | Total Time: 30 minutes | SERVES 4

6 garlic cloves
1 teaspoon olive oil
1 large cauliflower head, florets only
2 tablespoons duck or bacon fat
1½ teaspoons sea salt
1½ teaspoons freshly ground black pepper
1/3 cup (75ml/2½fl oz) almond milk

1. Preheat the oven to 425°F. Line two large baking sheets with parchment paper.
2. Make a little aluminum foil packet for the garlic. Taking a piece of foil, place the garlic in the middle, drizzle with oil, then fold two sides together and fold in both ends. Roast in the oven while you prepare the cauliflower.
3. In a large bowl, combine the cauliflower, duck or bacon fat, salt, and pepper and toss to coat.
4. Transfer to the prepared baking sheets and roast for 20 minutes.
5. Remove both the cauliflower and garlic from the oven. Transfer both to a food processor, add the almond milk, and puree until smooth. Enjoy!

CAL 130 | CAL FROM FAT 70 | TOTAL FAT 8G | SAT FAT 2.5G | SODIUM 800MG | FIBER 4G | PRO 4G

SALT & VINEGAR KALE CHIPS

These healthy chips are delicious, and they can actually be stored in an airtight container in a cool place if you have leftovers—though I think that's highly unlikely! These are essential for the busy Paleo family.

▶ Preparation Time: 5 minutes | Cooking Time: 20 minutes | Total Time: 25 minutes | SERVES 4

10 cups (670g/1½lbs) Tuscan, Russian Purple, curly, or plain kale, stemmed and torn into bite-size pieces
1 tablespoon olive oil
1 tablespoon unfiltered apple cider vinegar
1 teaspoon sea salt

1. Preheat the oven to 325°F. Line two large baking sheets with parchment paper.
2. In a large bowl, combine the kale, olive oil, and apple cider vinegar and toss well to coat.
3. Arrange in a single layer on the prepared baking sheets. Bake for 10 minutes, toss, then bake for another 10 minutes.
4. Once the kale is crispy and lightly browned, remove from the oven and season with salt. Allow to cool slightly before devouring!

CAL 120 | CAL FROM FAT 40 | TOTAL FAT 4.5G | SAT FAT 0.5G | SODIUM 550MG | FIBER 3G | PRO 6G

SAUTÉED SPINACH WITH GARLIC & CHILI

I've seen a lot of fancy ways to prepare spinach, but I really prefer spinach prepared simply because it highlights its naturally healthy and amazing taste. Why fuss? This one is a great side dish for pretty much any of the main dishes in this book.

▶ Preparation Time: 2 minutes | Cooking Time: 15 minutes, plus boiling time | Total Time: 17 minutes
SERVES 4

1½lbs (675g/24oz) baby spinach
1 teaspoon olive oil
3 garlic cloves, minced
1 teaspoon crushed red pepper flakes
½ to 1 teaspoon sea salt

1. Bring a large pot of water to a boil. Add the spinach and blanche for 30 seconds, or until the spinach turns bright green and wilts. Drain in a colander and press the water out with the back of a spoon.
2. Heat the olive oil in a large sauté pan over medium heat. Add the garlic, red pepper flakes, drained spinach, and salt and sauté for 30 seconds. Serve immediately.

CAL 100 | CAL FROM FAT 10 | TOTAL FAT 1G | SAT FAT 0G | SODIUM 340MG | FIBER 10G | PRO 5G

ROSEMARY GARLIC SPAGHETTI SQUASH FRITTERS

Spaghetti squash is incredibly versatile. Not only is it a Paleo-friendly substitute for pasta or rice, it also makes amazing fritters. With this dish, I often roast enough for the evening's meal and some extra for leftovers. Be sure to squeeze out the water from the squash so it turns crispy. Serve as an awesome side with a dish like the Quick Bison Chili (page 122), for a wonderful winter's night dinner.

▶ Preparation Time: 5 minutes | Cooking Time: 6–7 minutes | Total Time: 11–12 minutes | SERVES 4

2 cups (310g/11oz) Roasted Spaghetti Squash (page 144)
2 organic free-range eggs
¼ cup (25g/1oz) almond meal
2 garlic cloves, minced
1 tablespoon rosemary, chopped
1 teaspoon sea salt
1 teaspoon freshly ground black pepper
2 tablespoons olive oil, divided

1. Place the Roased Spaghetti Squash in a clean kitchen towel or a couple of paper towels and squeeze out as much liquid as possible.
2. In a medium bowl, combine the squash, eggs, almond meal, garlic, rosemary, salt, and pepper.
3. Heat 1 tablespoon oil in a large nonstick sauté pan over medium-high heat. Add ¼ cup (60ml) spoonfuls of batter and do not overcrowd the pan. Cook the fritters for 3–4 minutes, flip, and cook for another 3 minutes, or until golden. Transfer the fritters to a plate and keep warm. Add the remaining oil to the pan and cook the remainder of the batter.

CAL 160 | CAL FROM FAT 120 | TOTAL FAT 13G | SAT FAT 2G | SODIUM 530MG | FIBER 2G | PRO 5G

THAI GREEN CURRY VEGETABLES

The curry paste for this recipe is in the Make-Ahead chapter (page 201), and that helps make this dish so easy to prepare. Serve with a piece of grilled game or sautéed shrimp for a savory and satisfying dinner.

▶ Preparation Time: 10 minutes | Cooking Time: 7 minutes | Total Time: 17 minutes | SERVES 4

1 tablespoon sesame oil
¼ cup Green Curry Paste (page 201)
1 large red onion, sliced
3 cups (225g/80oz) sugar snaps, trimmed
1 red bell pepper, seeded and thinly sliced
1 yellow bell pepper, seeded and thinly sliced
1 x 14oz (400ml) can coconut milk
1 cup (240ml/8oz) vegetable broth
6 kaffir lime leaves
1 tablespoon raw honey
1 cup (30g/1oz) Thai basil
2 tablespoons coconut aminos
juice of 1 lime
½ teaspoon sea salt

1. Heat the oil in a large wok over medium-high heat.
2. Add the curry paste and stir about 30 seconds, or until fragrant.
3. Add the red onion, sugar snaps, bell peppers, coconut milk, vegetable broth, kaffir lime leaves, and honey. Stir to combine.
4. Reduce the heat to medium and simmer, stirring occasionally, for 5 minutes, or until vegetables are crisp-tender.
5. Remove from the heat and stir in the basil, coconut aminos, and lime juice. Season with salt and serve.

CAL 570 | CAL FROM FAT 220 | TOTAL FAT 25G | SAT FAT 19G | SODIUM 390MG | FIBER 4G | PRO 5G

CHAPTER 8

BAKED GOODS & DESSERTS

RAW CARROT CAKE BITES

Don't let the rawness put you off. Carrot cake is my favorite and this tastes pretty close to the real thing! They're perfectly portable and make a great take-along snack for a run, bike, or other workout. Best of all, they are the perfect portion size, calorically dense, and easily digestible.

▶ Preparation Time: 30 minutes | Cooking Time: 0 minutes | Total Time: 30 minutes | MAKES 8 BITES

6 Medjool dates, pitted
3 carrots, shredded
½ cup (50g/2oz) raw walnuts
½ cup (75g/2½oz) raw cashews
2 tablespoons Grade B maple syrup
1 teaspoon fresh ginger root, peeled and roughly chopped
¾ teaspoon cinnamon
¼ cup (20g/¾oz) shredded unsweetened coconut

1. Combine all ingredients except coconut in a food processor and process until smooth, about 1 minute.
2. Using a cookie scoop and damp hands, scoop out a tablespoon of batter and roll into a ball. Repeat with remaining batter.
3. Put the coconut on a small plate and roll the carrot cake balls in the coconut to coat. Refrigerate for 20 minutes before serving.

CAL 180 | CAL FROM FAT 70 | TOTAL FAT 8G | SAT FAT 1.5G | SODIUM 35MG | FIBER 3G | PRO 3G

NO-BAKE FIG & DATE COOKIES

These mid-workout snacks are simple to make, easy to carry, and tasty little balls of energy. They're my idea of a perfect treat!

▶ Preparation Time: 25 minutes | Cooking Time: 0 minutes | Total Time: 25 minutes
MAKES 8 COOKIES

10 dates, pitted
4 dried figs, stems removed
⅓ cup (33g/1¼oz) almond meal
2 tablespoons Grade B maple syrup

1. In a food processor, combine the dates, figs, and almond meal. Process 30 seconds, or until finely chopped and combined.
2. Drizzle in the maple syrup and pulse 10 times.
3. With a 1½-tablespoon scoop, scoop out the dough and roll into balls. (Wet your hands to prevent sticking).
4. Place the finished cookies in an airtight container and refrigerate for 20 minutes before serving. Keep refrigerated for up to one week.

CAL 80 | CAL FROM FAT 20 | TOTAL FAT 2.5G | SAT FAT 0G | SODIUM 0MG | FIBER 2G | PRO 1G

GRANOLA-STUFFED BAKED APPLES WITH APPLE CIDER SAUCE

This baked apple dessert, is simple and healthy and it can actually be eaten as a breakfast or a dessert. (I'll let you decide which you prefer!) The ideal baking apple should be firm and retain its shape when baked—I love Honeycrisp apples for stuffing and baking because they are wonderfully crisp, with a balance of sweet and tart flavors. The Granny Smith apple is also a great choice if you like apples extra tart.

▶ Preparation Time: 5 minutes | Cooking Time: 20–25 minutes | Total Time: 25–30 minutes | SERVES 4

4 Honeycrisp apples (or your favorite apples)
2 cups (245g/8½) Paleo-friendly granola
¼ cup (60ml/2fl oz) raw honey, melted
¼ cup (60ml/2fl oz) coconut butter, melted
1½ cups (350ml/12fl oz) fresh apple cider

1. Preheat the oven to 425°F. Line a 9" x 13" (10cm x 30cm) baking dish with aluminum foil.
2. Cut apples in half, cutting through the stem and bottom. Scoop out the core, seeds, and some of the pulp, leaving a ¼" (6mm)-thick shell. Place the apples in the prepared baking dish.
3. In a medium bowl, stir together the granola, honey, and coconut butter. Spoon the granola mixture into the apple halves. Pour the apple cider over the apples and cover with foil.
4. Bake in the oven for 10 minutes. Remove the foil and bake for another 10–15 minutes or until apples are tender.
5. To serve, transfer apples to a bowl and spoon the leftover liquid in the pan over them.

CAL 440 | CAL FROM FAT 190 | TOTAL FAT 22G | SAT FAT 16G | SODIUM 80MG | FIBER 6G | PRO 2G

FIG & ALMOND COOKIES WITH ORANGE ZEST

These are a twist on a traditional Italian cookie and the flavor combination works wonders together. Freeze the extra dough in pre-scooped balls, which you can pop in the oven for a quick and easy dessert.

▶ Preparation Time: 17 minutes | Cooking Time: 12–13 minutes | Total Time: 29–30 minutes
MAKES 32 COOKIES

1 cup (225g/8oz) dried figs, stems removed
½ cup (120ml/4fl oz) freshly squeezed orange juice
¾ cup (190g/7oz) coconut butter
¾ cup (144g/5oz) coconut sugar
1 organic free-range egg
1 teaspoon grated orange zest
2 cups (200g/7oz) almond meal
1 teaspoon ground cinnamon
½ teaspoon baking soda
½ teaspoon sea salt

1. Preheat the oven to 350°F. Line three baking sheets with parchment paper or silpats.
2. In a food processor, process the figs until finely chopped, about 30 seconds.
3. Turn on the food processor and pour in the orange juice. Process until combined.
4. Add the coconut butter and coconut sugar and process for 1 minute, or until whipped and well combined.
5. Add the egg and orange zest and pulse 10 times.
6. In a medium bowl, whisk together the almond meal, cinnamon, baking soda, and salt. Add to the food processor and process for another minute.
7. Using a 1½-tablespoon scoop, scoop the dough onto a prepared baking sheet. The cookie dough can be placed very close together since this is for freezing and not for baking.
8. Place the cookie dough in the freezer and freeze for 7 minutes.
9. Once the dough is frozen, transfer to the prepared baking sheets, spacing the dough 1" (2.5cm) apart. Bake in the oven for 12–13 minutes, or until the bottoms are lightly browned and the tops are set.

CAL 130 | CAL FROM FAT 80 | TOTAL FAT 9G | SAT FAT 5G | SODIUM 55MG | FIBER 1G | PRO 2G

PECAN SANDIES

Generally lighter and softer than traditional shortbread cookies, pecan sandies are an old-fashioned treat. This version is salty, sweet, chewy, and absolutely amazing!

▶ Preparation Time: 7 minutes, | Cooking Time: 10 minutes Total Time: 17 minutes | MAKES 20 COOKIES

2½ cups (250g/9oz) almond meal
1 cup (100g/3½oz) toasted pecans
¼ teaspoon baking soda
¼ teaspoon sea salt
½ cup (125g/4½oz) coconut butter, softened
⅓ cup (75ml/2½fl oz) raw honey
⅓ cup (75ml/2½fl oz) filtered water

1. Preheat the oven to 350°F. Line two baking sheets with parchment paper.
2. Combine the almond meal, pecans, baking soda, and salt in a food processor. Process for 10–20 seconds, or until the mixture is finely chopped.
3. Add the coconut butter, honey, and water and process for another 20 seconds, or until the dough pulls away from the sides and forms a ball.
4. Using a 1½-tablespoon scoop, scoop the dough onto a small cookie sheet lined with parchment paper. The cookie dough can be placed very close together since this is for freezing and not for baking.
5. Place the cookie dough in the freezer and freeze for 10 minutes.
6. Once the dough is frozen, transfer to the prepared baking sheet, spacing the dough 1" (2.5cm) apart. Bake in the oven for 10 minutes, or until lightly browned and set.
7. Bake in the oven for 10 minutes, or until lightly browned and set.

CAL 200 | CAL FROM FAT 160 | TOTAL FAT 18G | SAT FAT 6G | SODIUM 45MG | FIBER 2G | PRO 4G

ORANGE-ALMOND COCONUT MACAROONS

These are a Paleo-friendly take on traditional coconut macaroons. Feel free to switch up the orange zest for lemon or lime, or experiment with a combination of all three. As they are dry in texture, I often serve them with coffee to help moisten them up.

▶ Preparation Time: 10 minutes | Cooking Time: 15 minutes | Total Time: 25 minutes | MAKES 18 COOKIES

2 organic free-range egg whites, at room temperature
¼ cup (60ml/2fl oz) Grade B maple syrup
2 cups (160g/5½oz) unsweetened shredded coconut
½ cup (50g/1¾oz) almond meal
grated zest of 1 orange
¼ teaspoon sea salt

1. Preheat the oven to 350°F. Line a large baking sheet with parchment paper.
2. In a large bowl, beat the egg whites with a handheld mixer on high speed for about 2 minutes, or until light and foamy and stiff peaks form.
3. Gradually add the maple syrup and beat for another 1–2 minutes, or until the egg whites are glossy and firm (they will no longer hold a stiff peak because of the maple syrup, but should still hold medium peaks).
4. In a medium bowl, combine the coconut, almond meal, orange zest, and salt. Fold into the egg whites until incorporated. Do not overmix.
5. Using a 1½-tablespoon scoop, scoop the dough onto the prepared baking sheet, spacing the scoopfuls 1½" (4cm) apart. Bake in the oven for 15 minutes, or until they just begin to brown.
6. Serve warm or slightly cooled.

CAL 130 | CAL FROM FAT 80 | TOTAL FAT 9G | SAT FAT 6G | SODIUM 85MG | FIBER 2G | PRO 3G

LEMON POPPY SEED MINI MUFFINS

Whether you prefer them for breakfast or dessert, these muffins are light and refreshing. If you are making regular-sized muffins, simply increase the cooking time by 7 to 10 minutes.

▶ Preparation Time: 10 minutes | Cooking Time: 18–20 minutes | Total Time: 28–30 minutes
MAKES 36 MINI MUFFINS

2 cups (200g/7oz) almond meal
¾ cup (90g/3¼oz) coconut flour
1 tablespoon poppy seeds
1 teaspoon baking soda
½ teaspoon sea salt
¾ cup (175ml/6fl oz) raw honey, melted
⅔ cup (160ml/5½fl oz) coconut oil, melted
4 organic free-range eggs
⅔ cup (160ml/5½fl oz) coconut milk
grated zest and juice of 2 lemons

1. Preheat the oven to 350°F. Line enough mini muffin pans to make 36 muffins with mini muffin liners.
2. In a large bowl, combine the almond meal, coconut flour, poppy seeds, baking soda, and salt and mix well. Set aside.
3. In a food processor, combine the honey, coconut oil, eggs, coconut milk, lemon zest, and lemon juice. Process for one minute, or until well combined.
4. Add the wet ingredients to the dry ingredients and fold until just combined. Do not overmix.
5. Spoon the batter into the prepared muffin pans, filling the cups about three-quarters full.
6. Bake in the oven for 18–20 minutes, or until browned and a toothpick inserted into the center of a muffin comes out clean.

CAL 250 | CAL FROM FAT 160 | TOTAL FAT 18G | SAT FAT 10G | SODIUM 140MG | FIBER 3G | PRO 5G

FIG & PECAN COOKIES

Chewy and nutty, these delectable cookies are truly divine! And because of the coconut sugar, they taste like toasted marshmallows. If, by chance, there are any cookies left over, allow them to cool completely and store in an airtight container.

▶ Preparation Time: 5 minutes, | Cooking Time: 20 minutes | Total Time: 25 minutes | MAKES 20 COOKIES

1 cup (110g/4oz) chopped pecans
2 teaspoons grated orange zest
1 teaspoon cinnamon
¼ teaspoon sea salt
⅔ cup (100g/3½oz) dried figs, stems removed
2 organic free-range egg whites, at room temperature
1¾ cups (336g/11½oz) coconut sugar

1. Preheat the oven to 300°F. Line a large baking sheet with parchment paper.
2. In a food processor, combine the pecans, orange zest, cinnamon, and salt. Process for 30 seconds, or until finely ground. Transfer to a medium bowl.
3. Place the figs in a food processor and process for 30 seconds, or until finely chopped. Add the chopped figs to the pecan mixture.
4. In a large bowl, place the egg whites. Beat with a handheld mixer at high speed until stiff peaks form, about 2 minutes. Gradually add the sugar to the egg whites and beat at low speed until incorporated. Fold the pecan-fig mixture into the egg whites until just combined.
5. Using a 1½-tablespoon scoop, scoop the cookie dough onto the prepared baking sheet, spacing the scoopfuls 1½" (4cm) apart. Bake in the oven for 20 minutes, or until the bottom edges begin to brown.
6. Allow the cookies to cool for 5 minutes before serving.

CAL 290 | CAL FROM FAT 100 | TOTAL FAT 11G | SAT FAT 1G | SODIUM 85MG | FIBER 3G | PRO 3G

DARK CHOCOLATE ZUCCHINI BREAD

The pairing of rich chocolate and fresh zucchini makes this bread fluffy with a little denseness. It's a simple and delicious bread, which can be served straight from the oven or at room temperature. I like mine with a little almond butter—truly decadent!

▶ Preparation Time: 5 minutes | Cooking Time: 20–25 minutes | Total Time: 25–30 minutes
MAKES 2 MINI LOAVES

1 cup (250g/9oz) almond butter
3 tablespoons Grade B maple syrup
2 tablespoons dark cocoa powder
1½ teaspoons cinnamon
½ teaspoon sea salt
2 organic free-range eggs
1 large zucchini, shredded and excess water squeezed out
1 teaspoon unfiltered apple cider vinegar
½ teaspoon baking soda

1. Preheat the oven to 425°F. Grease two mini loaf pans and place them on a baking sheet.
2. In a medium bowl, combine the almond butter, maple syrup, cocoa powder, cinnamon, salt, and eggs. Beat with a handheld mixer on medium speed for 1 minute.
3. Stir in the zucchini.
4. In a small bowl, combine the apple cider vinegar and baking soda. (It will fizz up!). Add the baking soda mixture to the batter and stir to combine.
5. Divide the batter between the two loaf pans and bake for 20–25 minutes, or until a toothpick inserted in the center comes out clean.

CAL 250 | CAL FROM FAT 170 | TOTAL FAT 19G | SAT FAT 2G | SODIUM 290MG | FIBER 4G | PRO 10G

CHAPTER 9

MAKE-AHEAD RECIPES & CONDIMENTS

BANANA BREAD

Though total baking time is more than 30 minutes, this bread is great to make ahead and freeze or for use in Banana Bread French Toast (page 13). You may use yellow bananas for a less sweet version or riper bananas for a slightly sweeter bread. If using a glass pan versus a metal one, check the banana bread at around 35 minutes—baked goods tend to cook a little faster in glass than in metal. The best indicator to a fully cooked bread is always a well-browned top, a springy center when touched, and a toothpick that comes out of the bread with a few dry crumbs when inserted into the center.

▶ Preparation Time: 15 minutes | Cooking Time: 35–40 minutes | Total Time: 50–55 minutes | MAKES 1 LOAF

⅓ cup (80ml/2¾fl oz) coconut oil, plus extra for greasing
4 ripe bananas, mashed
4 organic free-range eggs
½ cup (125g/4½oz) unsalted almond butter
¼ cup (30g/1oz) coconut flour
¼ cup (25g/1oz) almond meal
1 tablespoon ground cinnamon
1 teaspoon baking soda
1 teaspoon baking powder (page 9)
¼ teaspoon sea salt

1. Preheat the oven to 350°F. Grease a 9" x 5" (23cm x 12cm) loaf pan with coconut oil.
2. In a stand-up mixer or food processor, combine the mashed bananas, eggs, almond butter, and coconut oil and blend until well incorporated. If using a food processor, transfer wet mixture to a large bowl.
3. In a medium bowl, combine the coconut flour, almond meal, cinnamon, baking soda, baking powder, and salt and mix well.
4. Using a wooden spoon, add the dry ingredients into the wet and mix until just combined, with a slightly lumpy consistency. Do not overmix.
5. Pour the batter into the greased loaf pan and bake for 35–40 minutes.
6. To test for doneness, insert a toothpick into the center and when it comes out nearly clean, your bread is done.
7. Flip the bread out of the pan onto a cooling rack. Allow to cool completely before slicing.

CAL 290 | CAL FROM FAT 180 | TOTAL FAT 20G | SAT FAT 8G | SODIUM 360MG | FIBER 5G | PRO 8G

PIZZA DOUGH

Several of my clients follow the Paleo lifestyle, and they were desperate for wonderful Paleo-friendly pizza dough. Trust me, this one will not disappoint! Feel free to create a combination of herbs and spices that you love. To make this ahead of time, freeze before rolling it out. This dough will keep in your freezer for up to one month. To thaw, transfer the frozen dough to your refrigerator and defrost overnight, or allow to sit at room temperature for 2 hours, or until thawed.

▶ Preparation Time: 7 minutes | Cooking Time: 7–9 minutes | Total Time: 14–16 minutes
MAKES 2 SMALL PIZZAS (6–8 slices each) or 1 LARGE PIZZA (12 slices)

1 cup (150g/5⅓oz) raw cashews
1 cup (100g/3½oz) almond meal
1 tablespoon Italian seasoning (or any combination of dried basil, parsley, rosemary, and thyme)
1 teaspoon granulated garlic
1 teaspoon sea salt
2 organic free-range eggs
2 tablespoons olive oil

1. Preheat the oven to 400°F. Line a baking sheet or two with parchment paper.
2. In a food processor, process the cashews to a flour-like consistency.
3. Add the almond meal, Italian seasoning, granulated garlic, and salt. Pulse five times to combine.
4. Add the eggs and olive oil. Pulse 10 times, or until combined. Allow the dough to sit for 5 minutes.
5. If making one large pizza, roll the dough into a ball. If making two small pizzas, separate the dough into two portions and roll both into balls. (Wet your hands to prevent sticking). Place the ball(s) of dough between two sheets of waxed paper. Roll to ¼" thick.
6. Transfer to the baking sheet and bake for 7–9 minutes, or until golden and crispy. If making one large pizza, check the crust after 7–9 minutes, and if needed, bake for another 2–4 minutes to ensure a crispy centre.
7. Top with your favorite toppings and sauce. If you like, use the Paleo-friendly Pizza Sauce on page 183.

CAL 230 | CAL FROM FAT 180 | TOTAL FAT 19G | SAT FAT 3G | SODIUM 260MG | FIBER 2G | PRO 8G

PIZZA SAUCE

This rich and delicious pizza sauce is super easy to prepare. Make a double batch ahead of time and freeze it for up to two months, then that last-minute pizza craving is a simple fix! Do the same with the Pizza Dough (page 182), and dinner will be on the table in no time.

▶ Preparation Time: 5 minutes | Cooking Time: 20 minutes | Total Time: 25 minutes
MAKES 2 CUPS | 16 SERVINGS (2 tablespoons per serving)

1 cup (250ml/9fl oz) tomato puree
¾ cup (175ml/7fl oz) tomato paste
4 garlic cloves, minced
1 teaspoon onion powder
1 teaspoon dried oregano
1 teaspoon dried basil
1 teaspoon dried parsley
1 teaspoon sea salt

1. Combine all ingredients in a medium heavy-bottomed saucepan. Bring to a boil over medium-high heat. Reduce heat to low and simmer for 20 minutes, stirring frequently.
2. Cool completely and store in an airtight container in the refrigerator for up to two weeks.

CAL 20 | CAL FROM FAT 0 | TOTAL FAT 0G | SAT FAT 0G | SODIUM 220MG | FIBER 1G | PRO 1G

HOMEMADE MARINARA

Even though this sauce takes more than 30 minutes to make, it is simmering on the stove for most of that time. Plus, homemade marinara is infinitely better than the jarred stuff! Take the time to make a big batch of this over a weekend and freeze it in small containers. When you're ready to use it, simply thaw in the refrigerator overnight and then pair it with one of your 30-minutes meals. You won't be sorry!

▶ Preparation Time: 5 minutes | Cooking Time: 2 hours 15 minutes | Total Time: 2 hours 20 minutes
MAKES 6 CUPS | 12 SERVINGS (½ cup per serving)

2 tablespoons olive oil
3 sweet onions, finely chopped
10 garlic cloves, minced
½ tablespoon dried basil
½ tablespoon dried parsley
1 teaspoon dried thyme
1 teaspoon dried rosemary
1 teaspoon dried oregano
2 x 28oz (800g) cans crushed tomatoes
2 cups filtered water
2 teaspoons sea salt
2 teaspoons freshly ground black pepper

1. Heat the olive oil in a large heavy-bottomed stockpot over medium heat.
2. Add the onions and sauté, stirring occasionally, for 10 minutes.
3. Add the garlic, basil, parsley, thyme, rosemary, and oregano and stir constantly for 30 seconds, or until very fragrant.
4. Add the crushed tomatoes and water, then increase to medium-high heat, and bring to a boil.
5. Reduce to medium-low heat and simmer for 2 hours, stirring occasionally to prevent the sauce from burning at the bottom.
6. Season with salt and pepper.
7. Cool completely and store in an airtight container in the fridge. This sauce will keep for up to two weeks in the fridge and up to two months in the freezer.

CAL 80 | CAL FROM FAT 25 | TOTAL FAT 2.5G | SAT FAT 0G | SODIUM 500MG | FIBER 3G | PRO 3G

WORCESTERSHIRE SAUCE

Worcestershire sauce is traditionally a fermented condiment used to season dishes like Caesar salads, hamburgers, and Bloody Marys. The store-bought version contains soy sauce, which is a no-no for the Paleo diet. This version is delicious and so simple to make. Use it to season your ground game and beef or add it to your favorite marinades for an additional depth of flavor.

▶ Preparation Time: 5 minutes | Cooking Time: 2 minutes | Total Time: 7 minutes
MAKES ⅔ CUP | 32 SERVINGS (1 teaspoon per serving)

½ cup (120ml/4fl oz) unfiltered apple cider vinegar
2 tablespoons filtered water
2 tablespoons coconut aminos
1 teaspoon anchovy paste
¼ teaspoon ground ginger
¼ teaspoon ground yellow mustard
¼ teaspoon onion powder
¼ teaspoon garlic powder
¼ teaspoon freshly ground black pepper
pinch of ground cinnamon

1. Place all ingredients in a small saucepan and whisk to combine.
2. Bring to a boil over medium-high heat, then reduce heat to low and simmer for 1–2 minutes.
3. Cool and store in a sterilized airtight container in the refrigerator for up to two months.

CAL 5 | CAL FROM FAT 0 | TOTAL FAT 0G | SAT FAT 0G | SODIUM 20MG | FIBER 0G | PRO 0G

HOMEMADE MAYONNAISE

There is no comparison between homemade and store-bought mayonnaise. Not only is this version easy to make, but it's so delicious, you will use it on any and everything your taste buds desire.

▶ Preparation Time: 6–12 minutes | Cooking Time: 0 minutes | Total Time: 6–12 minutes
MAKES 1 CUP | 16 SERVINGS (1 tablespoon per serving)

1 organic free-range egg yolk
½ teaspoon sea salt
½ teaspoon Dijon mustard
2 teaspoons lemon juice
1 teaspoon white wine vinegar
¾ cup (175ml/6fl oz) macadamia nut or avocado oil

1. In a large bowl, combine the egg yolk, salt, Dijon, lemon juice, and white wine vinegar. Whisk for 1–2 minutes, or until the yolk is thickened and light yellow.
2. In a slow stream, add in the oil, whisking vigorously to incorporate. This will take about 5–10 minutes, depending on your whisking skills.
3. Store in a sterilized airtight container in the refrigerator for one week.

CAL 100 | CAL FROM FAT 100 | TOTAL FAT 11G | SAT FAT 1.5G | SODIUM 65MG | FIBER 0G | PROTEIN 0G

SPICY HARISSA PASTE

Suited to use in marinades, soups, or with vegetables, harissa is an amazing Tunisian spice paste that is used as a condiment like ketchup. The spiciness of this particular paste can be adjusted by using different types of peppers.

▶ Preparation Time: 30 minutes | Cooking Time: 0 minutes | Total Time: 30 minutes
MAKES 1 CUP | 16 SERVINGS (1 tablespoon per serving)

8 dried guajillo chilies, stemmed
8 dried chile de árbol chilies, stemmed
1 serrano chili, stemmed and seeded
1 teaspoon caraway seeds
1 teaspoon cumin seeds
1 teaspoon coriander seeds
1 teaspoon dried mint
juice of 4 lemons
3 tablespoons olive oil
4 garlic cloves
1½ teaspoons sea salt

1. In a medium bowl, cover the dried chilies with boiling water and soak for 20 minutes.
2. In a small dry skillet over medium heat, add the caraway seeds, cumin seeds, and coriander seeds. Toast, stirring constantly, for 3–4 minutes, or until fragrant.
3. Using a pestle and mortar or spice grinder, combine the toasted spices and mint and pound or grind to a fine powder. Set aside.
4. Strain the chilies. In a food processor, combine the chilies, spices, lemon juice, olive oil, garlic, and salt. Puree until smooth.
5. Transfer to a sealable jar and refrigerate for up to one month.

CAL 90 | CAL FROM FAT 15 | TOTAL FAT 2G | SAT FAT 0G | SODIUM 25MG | FIBER 0G | PRO 3G

SIMPLE MUSTARD

This mustard is as simple as it comes. Try adding more vinegar, lemon juice, and herbs such as basil or tarragon. Store in a sterilized airtight container for up to three months.

▶ Preparation Time: 3 minutes | Cooking time: 0 minutes | Total Time: 3 minutes
MAKES ½ cup | 24 SERVINGS (1 teaspoon per serving)

½ cup (120g/4oz) mustard powder
½ cup (120ml/4fl oz) filtered water
1 teaspoon apple cider vinegar
¼ teaspoon sea salt

1. In a medium bowl, combine all ingredients and stir until smooth.
2. Allow to sit for 15 minutes before using.
3. Transfer to a sterilized airtight container and store in the refrigerator for up to three months.

CAL 15 | CAL FROM FAT 10 | TOTAL FAT 1G | SAT FAT 0G | SODIUM 35MG | FIBER 0G | PRO 1G

WHOLE-GRAIN MUSTARD

Adding herbs makes this an even better mustard. This will keep in an airtight container for up to three months.

▶ Preparation Time: 5 minutes | Cooking Time: 0 minutes | Total Time: 5 minutes
MAKES 1 CUP | 48 SERVINGS (1 teaspoon per serving)

¼ cup (45g/1½oz) yellow mustard seeds
¼ cup (45g/1½oz) brown mustard seeds
1 cup (240ml/8fl oz) white wine vinegar
4 teaspoons mustard powder
¼ cup (60ml/2fl oz) unfiltered apple cider vinegar
½ teaspoon sea salt

1. In a medium bowl, soak the yellow and brown mustard seeds in the white wine overnight.
2. Add all the ingredients into a food processor and process for 1 minute, or until smooth.
3. Transfer to a sterilized airtight container and refrigerate for four days before serving.

CAL 20 | CAL FROM FAT 5 | TOTAL FAT 1G | SAT FAT 0G | SODIUM 35MG | FIBER 0G | PRO 1G

BARBECUE SAUCE

Store-bought barbecue sauce is full of sugar and stabilizers . . . things we don't want to put into our bodies. This one takes some time to cook, but it is well worth the effort and also delicious to boot! If you like a spicier sauce, add more cayenne for a kicked-up version.

▶ Preparation Time: 10 minutes | Cook Time: 45 minutes | Total Time: 55 minutes
MAKES 2 CUPS | 16 SERVINGS (2 tablespoons per serving)

1 tablespoon olive oil or bacon fat
4 garlic cloves, minced
½ sweet onion, minced
¼ cup (60ml/2fl oz) unfiltered apple cider vinegar
2 tablespoons Dijon mustard
1 tablespoon raw honey
1 teaspoon sea salt
1 teaspoon coconut aminos
1 teaspoon sweet paprika
¼ teaspoon cayenne pepper
1½ cups (350ml/12fl oz) chicken broth
1 cup (235ml/9fl oz) tomato paste

1. Heat the oil or bacon fat in a large saucepan over medium heat.
2. Add the garlic and onion and sauté for 5–7 minutes, or until translucent and softened.
3. Add the apple cider vinegar, Dijon, honey, salt, coconut aminos, paprika, and cayenne to the pan and stir continuously for 30 seconds.
4. Add the chicken broth and tomato paste and stir until smooth.
5. Bring to a boil over medium-high heat, then reduce the heat, and simmer for 30–45 minutes, or until thickened. Allow to cool completely.
6. Store in a sterilized airtight container in the fridge for up to one week.

CAL 25 | CAL FROM FAT 5 | TOTAL FAT 0.5G | SAT FAT 0G | SODIUM 200MG | FIBER 1G | PROTEIN 0G

ASIAN ALMOND BUTTER DRESSING

This dressing was made for the Asian Chicken Salad (page 39), but it is so versatile and delicious that you will want to have extra in your fridge for salads, crudités, or even as a marinade for pork or chicken.

▶ Preparation Time: 5 minutes | Cooking Time: 0 minutes | Total Time: 5 minutes
MAKES 1½ CUPS | 24 SERVINGS (1 tablespoon per serving)

½ cup (125g/4½oz) unsalted almond butter
juice of 4 limes
⅓ cup (75ml/2 ½fl oz) Paleo-friendly fish sauce
2 tablespoons raw honey
2 tablespoons unfiltered apple cider vinegar
1 teaspoon crushed red pepper flakes

1. In a medium bowl, whisk together all ingredients.
2. Transfer to an airtight jar or container and store in refrigerator for up to two weeks.

CAL 80 | CAL FROM FAT 50 | TOTAL FAT 6G | SAT FAT 0G | SODIUM 650MG | FIBER 1G | PRO 3G

SIMPLE CUCUMBER RELISH

This relish is not only delicious, but also a great probiotic! This takes about two to five days to ferment and can be served with your favorite grilled meats—I especially love it with simple grilled sausage or even as a topper on the Lettuce-Wrapped Sausage Burgers (page 87).

▶ Preparation Time: 3 minutes | Cooking Time: 0 minutes | Total Time: 3 minutes
MAKES 1 CUP | 16 SERVINGS (1 tablespoon per serving)

4 large cucumbers, ends removed and roughly chopped
1 tablespoon dill
1 tablespoon mustard seeds
1 garlic clove
2 tablespoons sea salt
filtered water

1. In a food processor, combine all ingredients and pulse until finely chopped.
2. Transfer the mixture to a glass jar with a tight-fitting lid and pack it tightly using a wooden spoon. If there is not enough water occurring naturally from the mixture, cover with filtered water. You want the water to cover the mixture completely and still have 1" (2.5cm) of empty space from the top of the lid.
3. Seal tightly with the lid and leave in a warm place for 2–5 days. Taste the relish along the way to see if it's ready.
4. When ready, transfer the relish to the refrigerator and store for up to one week.

CAL 35 | CAL FROM FAT 0 | TOTAL FAT 0G | SAT FAT 0G | SODIUM 1200MG | FIBER 2G | PRO 2G

CREAMY HORSERADISH SAUCE

This divine sauce complements everything from beef and game to vegetables such as Spaghetti Squash Fritters (page 161). The amount of horseradish can be altered to fit your spicy desires, but bear in mind that a little goes a long way.

▶ Preparation Time: 5 minutes | Cooking Time: 0 minutes | Total Time: 5 minutes | MAKES 1½ CUPS
24 SERVINGS (1 tablespoon per serving)

1 organic free-range egg
¼ teaspoon mustard powder
1 tablespoon freshly squeezed lemon juice
1 cup (240ml/8fl oz) olive oil
1 cup grated horseradish
2 tablespoons unfiltered apple cider vinegar
½ teaspoon sea salt

1. In a blender, mix the egg, mustard powder, and lemon juice on low speed until well blended.
2. Slowly drizzle in the olive oil and blend until the oil is completely incorporated and no longer visible. You should have a creamy mayonnaise base.
3. Transfer the mayonnaise to a medium bowl and stir in the horseradish, vinegar, and salt.
4. Store in an airtight container in the refrigerator for up to two weeks.

CAL 110 | CAL FROM FAT 100 | TOTAL FAT 11G | SAT FAT 1.5G | SODIUM 85MG | FIBER 0G | PRO 0G

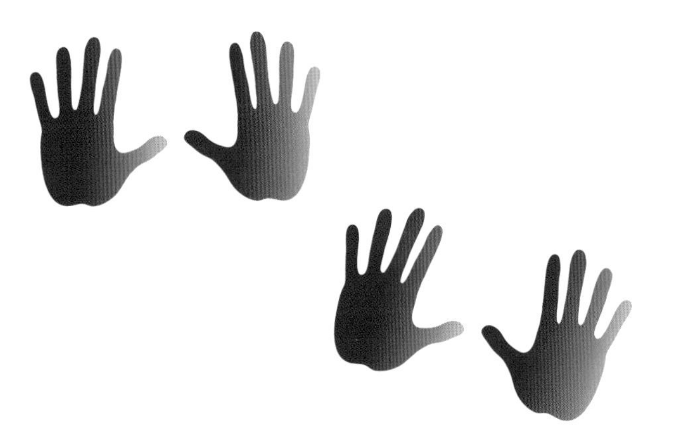

HOT PEPPER SAUCE

Everyone loves Sriracha, and this recipe comes as close as you'll get to the real thing. It can replace any hot sauce in any recipe. If you like a spicier sauce, leave in some of the jalapeño ribs and seeds.

▶ Preparation Time: 5 minutes | Cooking Time: 10 minutes | Total Time: 15 minutes
MAKES 2 CUPS | 48 SERVINGS (2 teaspoons per serving)

1½lbs (675g/24oz) red jalapeños, stemmed, seeded, and roughly chopped
10 garlic cloves, smashed
½ cup (120ml/4fl oz) unfiltered apple cider vinegar
¼ cup (75ml/2fl oz) raw honey
3 tablespoons tomato paste
2 tablespoons Paleo-friendly fish sauce
2 teaspoons sea salt

1. In a food processor or blender, combine all the ingredients and puree until smooth.
2. Transfer the puree to a medium heavy-bottomed saucepan and bring to a boil over medium-high heat. Reduce the heat to low and simmer for 10 minutes, stirring occasionally.
3. Transfer the sauce to a glass jar with a tight-fitting lid and allow to cool completely, uncovered, about 2 hours.
4. Seal with the lid and store in the refrigerator for up to one month.

CAL 20 | CAL FROM FAT 0 | TOTAL FAT 0G | SAT FAT 0G | SODIUM 580MG | FIBER 1G | PRO 1G

Roland

LEMON, CAPER & ANCHOVY SAUCE

Don't be thrown off by the combination of lemon, capers, and anchovies—the salty and tart flavors are a perfect pairing and add a new dimension to steamed veggies, grilled chicken, and baked fish.

▶ Preparation Time: 5 minutes | Cooking Time: 5 minutes | Total Time: 10 minutes
MAKES 1 CUP | 24 SERVINGS (2 teaspoons per serving)

1 x 2oz (50g) can anchovy fillets, packed in olive oil
½ cup (120ml/4fl oz) olive oil
1 teaspoon crushed red pepper flakes
4 tablespoons capers, drained
juice of 2 lemons
¼ cup (10g/¼oz) parsley leaves, chopped

1. In a food processor, finely mince the anchovies.
2. In a small saucepan, combine the anchovies, olive oil, and red pepper flakes and mix well. Bring to a boil over medium-high heat, then reduce heat to low and simmer for 5 minutes, or until the anchovies have completely dissolved in the oil.
3. In the meantime, add the capers to the food processor and pulse until finely chopped.
4. When the anchovies have finished cooking, remove from heat. Stir in the capers, lemon juice, and parsley.
5. Cool completely and then store in an airtight container in the refrigerator for up to one week.

CAL 90 | CAL FROM FAT 90 | TOTAL FAT 10G | SAT FAT 1.5G | SODIUM 140MG | FIBER 0G | PRO 1G

HOMEMADE KETCHUP

This isn't a 30-minute recipe, but if you have never tried homemade ketchup before, you're in for a real treat. This ketchup is full of fresh tomatoes, spices, aromatics, and love. Use this as you would the traditional condiment and feel good about putting it on those amazing Spicy Baked Sweet Potato Fries (page 155), Carrot Fries with Avocado Aioli (page 150), or Buffalo Burger with Caramelized Onions, Mushrooms & Lettuce (page 127).

▶ Preparation Time: 10 minutes | Cook Time: up to 2 hours 12 minutes | Total Time: up to 2 hours 22 minutes
MAKES 2 CUPS | 32 SERVINGS (1 tablespoon per serving)

1 tablespoon olive oil
1 large sweet onion, chopped
1 small fennel bulb, chopped
1 celery rib, chopped
1 teaspoon minced ginger
2 garlic cloves, chopped
½ jalapeño, seeded and chopped
1 tablespoon coriander seeds
1 teaspoon sea salt
1 teaspoon freshly ground black pepper
1½ cups (350ml/12fl oz) filtered water
1lb (450g/16oz) plum tomatoes, chopped
2 cups (480g/17oz) canned plum tomatoes
1 cup (40g/1½oz) basil leaves
¾ to 1 cup (175 to 240ml/6 to 8fl oz) unfiltered apple cider vinegar, to taste

1. Heat the olive oil in a large saucepan over medium-high heat.
2. Add the onion, fennel, celery, ginger, garlic, jalapeño, coriander seeds, salt, and pepper and mix well.
3. Reduce heat to medium-low and cook, stirring occasionally, for about 12 minutes, or until the vegetables have softened.
4. Add the water and tomatoes. Bring to a boil, then reduce the heat and simmer for 45–60 minutes. Loosely cover with a lid to prevent splattering and allow for the water to reduce and the flavors to develop.
5. Pour the ketchup into a blender, add basil, and process until smooth.
6. Strain the sauce through a sieve, then pour it into a clean saucepan.
7. Add the vinegar according to taste and simmer for 30–60 minutes, depending on the desired consistency. Adjust the seasoning to taste.
8. Cool completely, then transfer to a sterilized airtight container and. refrigerate for up to six months.

CAL 20 | CAL FROM FAT 5 | TOTAL FAT 0.5G | SAT FAT 0G | SODIUM 100MG | FIBER 1G | PRO 1G

GREEN CURRY PASTE

This curry paste is so tasty! But even better than being tasty, it's so good for you too! Curry has been shown to reduce the risk of Alzheimer's, dementia, and cancer, while boosting immunity, easing digestion, and helping to burn fat.

▶ Preparation Time: 10 minutes | Cooking Time: 0 minutes | Total Time: 3 hours 10 minutes with sitting time
MAKES 1 CUP | 16 SERVINGS (1 tablespoon per serving)

1 shallot, quartered
1 x 6" (15cm) piece lemongrass, outer leaves discarded and roughly chopped
1 to 2 Hatch or bird's eye red chilies, or ½ to 1 teaspoon cayenne pepper
4 garlic cloves
1 x 2" (5cm) piece fresh ginger root, peeled
3 tablespoons ghee or coconut oil
2 tablespoons tomato paste
2 tablespoons anchovy paste
2 tablespoons chili powder
1 tablespoon raw honey or coconut nectar
1 teaspoon ground cumin
1 teaspoon ground coriander
¼ teaspoon freshly ground black pepper
¼ teaspoon ground cinnamon
juice of 1 lime

1. Place all ingredients in a food processor and process for 1 minute, or until smooth.
2. Transfer to an airtight container and allow to sit at room temperature for 2–3 hours before using. This allows the flavors to develop in the curry paste.
3. If not using immediately, store in the refrigerator for up to three months.

CAL 40 | CAL FROM FAT 25 | TOTAL FAT 3G | SAT FAT 2.5G | SODIUM 140MG | FIBER 0G | PRO 1G

INDEX

INDEX